REFLECTIONS

FROM GOD'S STORY OF HOPE

The Bible's Big Story in Word & Image

Good Soil Evangelism & Discipleship
Email: Info@GoodSoil.com
Web: www.GoodSoil.com
Phone: (877) 959-2293

Association of Baptists for World Evangelism
P.O. Box 8585
Harrisburg, PA 17105 USA

Author - Gil Thomas
Art Direction & Design - Justinen Creative Group
Interior Illustrations - Lars Justinen, Steve Creitz, Marcus Mashburn, Aric Nicholson

Printed in China.

15 16 17/CTPS/04 03 02

ISBN 978-1-888796-59-9

REAL PEOPLE

I had a hard day at work, so I eased down onto the couch and flipped the TV on. But then I heard them: little feet padding up the stairs. Then soft voices on the other side of the door: "Grandpa! Grandpa! I'm coming!" I turned the TV off and waited. Before long they burst through the door.

"Grandpa, Grandpa!" Maddie exclaimed with glee as she bounced into the living room, across the floor, and into my arms. Little Lexi waddled along behind struggling to keep her balance in all the excitement. She, too, gave me a hug and then headed straight for the bookshelf—the low one within her reach which we keep stocked with books for just such occasions. She brought some books over to Grandpa. My grandchildren climbed into my lap, and we began to read. This is a scene we've repeated dozens of times. I loved reading to my children, and now I love reading to my grandchildren.

One of the books Lexi brought me started with "Once upon a time," and we were off into an imaginary world—and why not? There are many such good stories with valuable lessons which we read to our children and grandchildren. But how much better it is to read about real people struggling with real problems as they journey through life! And even better: stories about those real people given to us by the one, true and living God. (By the way, the books Lexi invariably picks over all the others are Bible storybooks.)

The book you hold in your hands tells true stories about real people living in real places in real time. The events comprise a large part of God's story of hope starting with the beginning of time and continuing through to the future. You will read happy stories and sad stories; stories of victory and stories of defeat; stories of love and compassion and stories of hatred and deceit; stories of people coming to and having communion with their Creator; stories of people running away from God. But throughout you will see a God who loves people, gives hope, and provides a way back to Him. You will read about issues we all want our children to ponder as they go through life because the stories are about real people and real-life experiences.

So is this a book for children or for adults? Yes! *Reflections* can be read to and by children, but adults can read and meditate upon its truths as well. Adults are more prepared to reason through the deeper meanings. They can ask why and consider how. All readers and listeners can examine the beautiful, lifelike images, imagine the emotions the characters may have experienced, and contemplate the implications for life here and now.

Whether you read these stories to children or for your own enlightenment, our desire is that you reflect on God's story of hope. Let the story invade your life. It doesn't start with "Once upon a time," but with the creation of time. And it doesn't end with "… and they all lived happily ever after," but it does end happily for some, and it could for you.

REAL PLACES

THE ANCIENT NEAR EAST

4

THE HOLY LAND
CANAAN/PALESTINE

These maps are included so you can see where these real events happened to real people. Many places mentioned in the stories are marked on the maps. Take advantage of them. For example, if you read that someone traveled from Ur to Haran, or from Jerusalem to Bethany, look back at the maps; see how far they may have traveled. Try to get a sense of what it must have been like to travel that distance, or live near that lake or river, or climb that mountain. The maps are "value-added" to aid in your understanding of the stories.

5

REAL TIME

Since these stories are actually about true events that happened many years ago (and will happen in the future), it is helpful to show their relation to one another. They can be divided into 25 eras— distinct periods of time as shown by these colored ribbons. As you read, note these eras as markers in time to gain a better understanding of when these people lived and when these events transpired.

ARRIVAL
SECLUSION
POPULARITY
OPPOSITION
SUFFERING
VICTORY
APOSTLES
CHURCH
TRIBULATION
KINGDOM
JUDGMENT
RESTORATION

The Eternal God

Nothing.
No thing.

No light, no color, no shape or sound.
Really nothing at all around.
It isn't hot, it isn't cold,
Really—if I may be so bold—
There's nothing positive to see,
But negative also cannot be.

Before the mountains or the seas,
Before the flowers and the trees,
Before the sky, the stars, the sun—
Before existed even one
Of what we call "person, place or thing"
Or little birds began to sing—

Spirit-being—no body there
About to speak into (no) air
The self-existing Mighty One
Who, self-sufficient, needs no one,
No thing. Don't think it odd,
In the beginning, God …

It's hard for us to imagine, but at one time nothing existed. There was nothing to see or hear. That means you couldn't go to the beach and swim, or climb a mountain, hear the roar of a waterfall, or even listen to a tiny bird sing. Nothing existed and there was nothing to do. But no one minded, because there weren't any people either!

Back then, before time began, only God existed. Imagine what that would be like for you—being the only one around. No one to talk to, except yourself. No one with whom you can take a walk. No one to play games with—you are the only one! How would you like that?

Well, God didn't mind. You see, He is self-sufficient. What does that mean? It means that He didn't (and He still doesn't) need anyone. He is perfect and perfectly complete in Himself. He can be at peace, content, confident, secure, and fulfilled just by existing. Now that is perfection.

God is also self-existent. The dictionary says that self-existent means "existing independently of any cause" or "having an independent existence." We can't say that about ourselves. Without our parents, we wouldn't be here. No one did anything to bring about God's existence. He had no parents, no creator.

Who is this God? In the very beginning of the Bible we see that He is called Elohim. That's the plural form of god in Hebrew used in its ordinary sense, but it is specifically used in the plural with singular verbs to refer to the supreme God. Elohim is clearly someone special—more than special. He is so singularly special that one has to use the plural to refer to Him.

As we continue to read we see that He is spirit. He doesn't have a body. Since He doesn't have a body, He is not limited by time and space and matter.

In another part of the Bible we see—but wait. Let's not get ahead of ourselves. We want to learn God's story starting from the beginning and going right through to the end. Let's learn more about God (Elohim) bit by bit as He reveals Himself in the Bible. For now, we'll be satisfied knowing that Elohim, powerful, self-existent, never-created God, was around before anything else.

In the beginning, God …

In its opening statement, the Bible addresses the most basic issue of human existence by declaring that the something or someone who has always existed is God.

OLD TESTAMENT

CREATION
FALL
FLOOD
BABEL
PATRIARCHS
MOSES
JOSHUA
JUDGES
MONARCHY
DIVISION
EXILE
RETURN

Creation of Angels

Before time, or space, or light, or anything existed, Elohim (Almighty God), existing in perfect communion and harmony with Himself, determined that He would create. In His unlimited wisdom, He looked down through the corridors of time which had not yet begun and the future of the yet uncreated universe and crafted the blueprints not only of people and animals and worlds and stars, but of a plan that would glorify Him and bring great joy to all His created beings.

When His purpose was established, his intentions set, the strategy complete, God began to create. And He started with highly intelligent, holy spirit-beings we call angels. He created thousands and thousands and millions and millions of them. He created them with differing levels of authority and power. Some He created for one purpose, some for another.

Now even though Heaven, the place where God dwells, is their home, these fantastic spirit-beings have access to earth where they can appear and disappear suddenly. When they appear, sometimes they appear with wings, other times without. Even though they can move quickly and are very powerful, angels, created by God, are subject to His control.

The first movement of God's symphony of creation, which was about to bring into existence amazing wonders, began with angels, whom He created to serve and worship Him forever. But in His desire for service which would flow from love for Him, God added to the angels' long list of attributes one more: choice.

In what was probably His first act as a Creator, the God of the Bible created spirit-beings that we call "angels."

Creation of the Universe

Now with an audience to see and hear the unfolding symphony of creation, God turned the page of the music and lifted His baton. He had laid the foundations of the earth and marked out the horizon. Silence now reigned, anticipation. As a hush came over the angels, God spoke.

"Light!" And light appeared. God made the light to be beneficial, and He separated the light from the darkness. He gave a name to the light: Day. And He gave a name to the darkness: Night. And there it was: the first evening and the first morning—Day One of creation.

Then, "Space!" God spoke again. "Space, appear between the waters below and the waters above." In that way, God separated the waters on earth from waters above the earth, and He gave a name to the space: Sky. And there it was: the second evening and the second morning—Day Two of creation.

God spoke again. "Waters, come together. Dry land, appear." And it happened! God gave a name to the land, Earth, and a name to the waters, Oceans, and He saw to it that they were beneficial. Then God said, "Grow out of the ground, plants! All you seed-bearing plants, and all you fruit-bearing trees with seeds, grow!" And up from the ground, all kinds of beautiful plants with green leaves and all sorts of colorful flowers began to break through the ground. And growing right past the plants up into the sky grew trees with fruit—so many different shapes and colors! God made all the plants to be beneficial. That was the third evening and the third morning—Day Three of creation.

Then God said, "Lights, appear! Shine in the sky above and separate Night from Day. Mark seasons and days and years and give light to Earth." And it happened just as He said. God made two principal lights—the greater to shine throughout the day and the lesser to shine throughout the night with all the shining, twinkling stars—millions and billions of bright stars. He placed these lights in the heavenly sky to shine on Earth and to separate the light from the dark. God knew that the lights were beneficial, and the fourth evening and morning came to a close—Day Four of creation.

Then God said, "Ocean, be filled with fish and all kinds of sea creatures. Birds, fly through Sky over Earth." That's how God created sea creatures—large and small and all kinds of birds. From huge whales to tiny plankton, they appeared and began swimming through the water; some jumped and splashed as they landed. Large birds and small of all different colors appeared and began flying through the sky. God knew they were all beneficial; and He blessed them, saying, "Prosper! Reproduce! Fill Ocean, sea creatures! Birds, reproduce on Earth." Evening passed and morning—Day Five of creation.

Again God spoke: "Earth, generate life—all kinds—cattle and reptiles and wild animals!" And just like the other times, it happened. Huge animals and tiny creatures appeared and began moving about on the earth. Their shapes were oh so different one from the other. And oh, the sounds they created! Roaring and neighing and braying and barking and meowing and elephants blowing their horns! What a symphony of praise to almighty God!

God created every kind of wild animal and reptile and bug—large and minute—and He saw that it was all beneficial.

God also created the universe, including our earth and its heavens, as well as its living organisms—plants and animals of all kinds.

Creation of Mankind

The sixth day was not over yet. God spoke again, this time to Himself. He said, "Let us make human beings—male and female—in our image, reflecting our nature and able to be responsible for the fish in Ocean, the birds in Sky, and the cattle and all the animals moving about on Earth."

So the eternal, self-existent, almighty God reached down and formed Man from the dirt of Earth; then He breathed into his nostrils the breath of life. At that moment, Man came alive—a living soul!

Then God planted a beautiful garden in the east with all kinds of trees and placed Man in the garden to care for it, to work the ground, and to keep it in order. God spoke again, saying, "It is not beneficial for Man to be alone. I will make him a helper, a companion." (Remember that God had already planned to make human beings— male and female.) So God brought all the animals he made to Man so that he could name them. Man gave names to all the animals and birds, but Man did not find a suitable companion for himself.

So God put Man into a deep sleep. As he slept God removed one of Man's ribs and closed up his flesh. Then God built up around the rib into a beautiful female and presented her to Man.

Then Man said,

> Finally! One who was made from my bone,
> Is there a being like me? She alone!
> Oh what shall I call this one at my hand?
> She shall be Woman; she was taken from Man.

Man and Woman were totally at ease and comfortable with each other just as God had made them—*au naturel*. God placed these unique beings that uniquely reflected His nature in the garden and blessed them: "Prosper! Reproduce! Fill Earth! Take charge! Be responsible for the fish in the sea and the birds in the air and every living thing that moves on the earth." He continued, saying, "Look! I have given you every plant and the fruit of all the trees to eat and gain nourishment. All the animals shall also eat from all the plants that grow from the ground."

God saw to it that all was beneficial and worthwhile. And there it was, evening and morning—Day Six of creation.

Then God created a man and a woman, Adam and Eve, and commissioned them to rule over His earthly creation.

Life in Paradise

The garden God had planted in the east was a beautiful, protected place called Eden.[1] The garden had all kinds of wonderful-looking (and tasting!) fruit trees. Right in the middle of the garden God planted two special trees: the Tree of Life and the Tree of the Knowledge of Good and Evil. The garden was well watered because a river bubbled up and flowed out of the garden, dividing up into four rivers! Imagine the beautiful trees and plants and the crystal-clear water flowing through paradise. Wouldn't it be wonderful to live there?

God placed the man and woman He had made in that breathtaking, luscious paradise and told them to take care of it. They were in charge! He had already told them to prosper, reproduce, and fill Earth, taking charge of it. Now they also had the responsibility of caring for God's beautiful, special garden.

It's hard to imagine what it was like or how beautiful the garden was. But I'm sure that as the man and the woman walked around in the garden, they were filled with wonder and awe, and their hearts and mouths were filled with praise to God. I'm sure they enjoyed their work, too, as they took care of this garden for their Creator.

When God placed them in the garden, He told them to eat of any and all of the trees—except for one: the Tree of the Knowledge of Good and Evil. God told them that if they would eat from that tree, they would die. But think of it: apples, peaches, mangoes, cherries, oranges, lemons, limes, pomegranates, cashews, bananas—and many more—all at hand to enjoy as much as they wanted. This Eden truly was a paradise. And to add to it, the man and woman carried on a close, personal relationship with their Creator God.

---

1 The Hebrew word for Eden means "delight, pleasure, or abundant fertility" while "paradise" (an old Persian word meaning "enclosed park, pleasure ground") was used in a later Greek version of the Bible for Eden.

Adam and Eve lived in the beautiful paradise Garden of Eden with abundant freedom and pleasures and only one rule to obey.

Fall of a Powerful Angel

Now, some time after God had created the angels and yet before the creation of man and woman, something terrible had happened—something that would affect everyone and every created thing in God's wonderful universe.

God had created one of the angels more beautiful than all the others. At one point God said to this angel,

You were …
Perfect in wisdom, perfect in beauty
Walking my mountain performing your duty.
An angel so special, sparkling like gold,
And silver, precious stones—elegance untold.

How marvelous this angel must have been! We can't even imagine. But something happened. The angel became proud and corrupt because of its great beauty.

This angel said,

I will ascend to Heaven and there I will raise my throne
Higher than all God's stars above and I will sit alone!
Presiding over all the gods on that utmost of heights,
I'll be the brightest of the lights, I'll be the sight of sights.
I will ascend above the clouds—the very tops of them.
I'll make myself like the Most High and never bow again!

So God punished that angel who became known as Satan, the Devil. The Most High God said, "From the day I created you, you were blameless—until that day that evil was found in you," and He drove Satan from His presence.

Satan wanted to rise higher and higher, but God threw him down. Down to the grave, down to the depths of the pit.

At some earlier time, one of God's most powerful and beautiful angels led other angels in a failed rebellion against God and became known as Satan, the Devil.

Beginning of Human Sin

Satan rebelled, wanting to be like God, and he was judged. Now God had created Man and Woman in His own image and placed them in His garden. They were getting special attention. I'm sure Satan was not happy about this.

Remember that God had told Man that he could eat from any and all trees of the garden except for one. Satan developed a plan to use that command to his advantage. First, he would misquote God just enough to make Him seem unloving. Then he would deny that God would—or even could—punish disobedience as He had promised. Then he would suggest that God only gave this warning because He is selfish and jealous. He probably thought, "This is going to be good." He was ready to put his plan into action.

Satan appeared to Eve in the form of a serpent and said, "Is it true that God told you not to eat from any of the trees in the garden?" The woman replied, "Of course not! God told us we could eat from all but one of the trees; and that one we can't even touch or we will die!"

"You won't die," the serpent jeered. "God knows that when you eat from this tree, you will be able to understand the difference between good and evil just like He does!"

The woman listened to the serpent. She looked at the fruit. The fruit looked tasty enough, tantalizingly so.

She thought about what the serpent had said. If she ate the fruit, could she really know more? Could she know as much as God knew? It made sense to her, so she took a piece and ate it. Then she turned and gave some to her husband, and he ate it, too.

Satan's plan succeeded. He was able to get the man and the woman to disobey God. I imagine he was pretty happy and was eager to see what God would do about it.

Disobedience—any instance of not doing what God commands—is called sin. This first disobedience of Man and Woman which resulted in some severe long-term consequences is generally called the "Fall of Man" or simply "The Fall."

In continued defiance against God, Satan enticed the woman to eat of the forbidden tree, and the woman then influenced Adam to do the same thing, in spite of God's clear and loving warning.

Origin of Death

All of a sudden the man and woman did see something they hadn't noticed before: they were naked! And they knew something they hadn't known before: they were embarrassed to be walking around like that. They didn't know what to do, but they tried plucking fig leaves from a tree and tying them together to make some kind of clothes for themselves. What they didn't realize is that big, beautiful, soft, green leaves shrivel up and die soon after they are no longer attached to the tree. But for now, it seemed to work.

Then the first man and his wife heard God moving about in the garden in the cool evening breeze. They quickly hid among the trees of the garden.

"Where are you?" God called out to the man.

"I … uh … I heard you in the garden, and I was afraid because I was naked; so I hid."

"Who told you that you were naked? Did you eat the fruit from the tree of which I told you not to eat?"

"Well, that woman you gave me as a companion—she gave me the fruit, and I ate it."

So God asked the woman, "What have you done?"

The woman said, "Serpent tricked me; that's why I ate it."

When Adam and his wife disobeyed (sinned) that day, the gradual process of physical death began to work in their bodies. The Bible tells us later that Adam lived a total of 930 years, and then he died. He did eventually experience the penalty of physical death. But on the very day they sinned, Adam and his wife died spiritually. Even though God was right there with them, they had a rift in their relationship; they were separated from God. Their right relationship with Him had become tarnished.

And on that very day when Adam first disobeyed God, sin and death entered the world and so would infect all mankind. We all sin and we all die as judgment for our sin.

Because God is a holy and just judge, Adam and the woman suffered the consequences of their disobedience; they immediately died spiritually and eventually died physically.

Promise of a Satan Conqueror

But that day wasn't over yet. God had a few words to say—in judgment. However, it wasn't all bad news. In fact, some of it was good news, very good news.

God, the Judge, started by speaking to the snake. Now remember, the snake is possessed by Satan at this point. God said, "Because of your involvement in this, you are cursed more than all of the other animals, domestic and wild. You are cursed to slither around on your belly and eat dirt as long as you live." Does that mean that snakes had legs and feet before this? I'm not sure, but it certainly is possible. The fact that all created beings were cursed at the same time to a somewhat lesser degree becomes clear further on in God's big story.

As God continues, He seems to address a different audience; He seems to speak directly to Satan within the snake.

"I am declaring war between you and Woman, between your descendant and her descendant. He will stomp on your head, and you will bruise his heel."

Wow! Until now, this had been a very bad day. Adam and his wife had learned that God's warning about the consequences of disobedience had been accurate. Even though Satan had tried to convince Woman that God was keeping something from her, he (Satan) had been the liar and deceiver; God had been truthful. Now, revealing that He loves His people in spite of the bad things they do, God gives a promise of good news: a future descendant of the woman would strike the deathblow to Satan and his spiteful plans against God and humans.

Even though Adam and his wife may not have understood all of the ramifications of this good-news promise at this early stage, I'm sure they were somewhat encouraged. But the punishment wasn't over yet. God, the Judge, had to deal with two more culprits. That would be less encouraging.

God then promised that a special offspring of the woman would someday conquer Satan because of Satan's evil participation in Adam and the woman's disobedience.

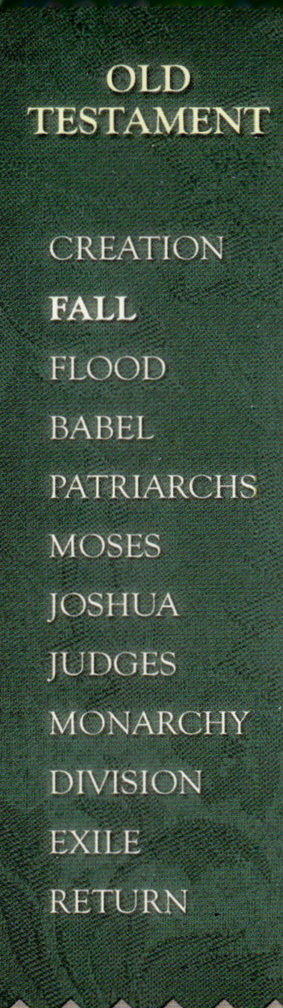

Sin's Extensive Effects

When Adam and his wife took that fateful bite, they could not have imagined the trouble they were bringing on themselves and all of creation. They were about to find out as God pronounced His judgment. But only over the years to come, as the sentence played out, would they truly experience the agony and grief caused by that choice.

After dealing with the serpent, God turned to the woman.

"Trouble
Will multiply
In your pregnancies
From conception to birth:
Discomfort, twinges of pain, aching spasms, deep pangs of distress."

That was enough: to have to suffer during an act as natural, wondrous, and glorious as bringing a baby—a product of the love of man and woman—into being. But there was more. God continued.

"You will long and desire and crave to rule
Your husband, but he will rule over you."

There it was: the beginning of conflict in marriage. That was God's punishment for disobedience meted out to the woman. Then He turned to Adam.

"Since you listened to your wife and ate from the tree I told you not to eat from,

It's your fault that the ground is cursed,
Getting food from it will make you thirst!
Thorns and thistles will come up with ease.
But produce food? Get on your knees
And work and sweat—yes, all day long!
Till, sow, harvest, coax plants along,
But still one day you will go down
Into the ground under a mound
Of dirt. That's where you started out.
And there you'll end, without a doubt."

Even though God did not curse the man and the woman as He did the snake, He cursed the ground and all creation with it. Producing food from the earth was going to be difficult now. When God created the universe and all that was in it, it was "beneficial." Man's disobedience brought about the dissolution of the earth's perfectly balanced ecosystem. Now all of creation has to go through a frustrating time—almost like the birth pangs of the woman— waiting for some kind of redemption; some kind of hope. And that hope would only come through the promised one.

But the problems caused by Adam and the woman's sin would affect God's creation in many negative ways for generations to come, including burdensome toil and miserable pain.

Provision of Coverings

You know how husbands and wives sometimes have arguments? Many times they argue about the same thing, over and over again. I wonder how many times Adam and his wife fought over eating the forbidden fruit, over whose fault it was. Of course we don't know, but interestingly enough the very first thing Adam did, after hearing God's pronouncement of judgment for his disobedience and that of his wife, was not to argue with her.

Instead, Adam responded in faith to God's promises. Promises? Yes. God promised the woman that He would multiply the trouble in her pregnancies, right? So, it was going to hurt, but Adam's wife was going to have babies, lots of them! That was a promise! God had also promised Satan that a descendant of the woman would stomp on his head. Not only would Adam's wife have babies, but one day a descendant of hers would deliver them from the death-bringer, Satan. Adam responded to this by naming his wife Eve (which sounds like "life-giver"[2]). The one he originally called woman (for she was taken from man) now had a beautiful new name that would always remind them of God's promises to give life in more ways than one: in the form of little babies and by providing a Deliverer from death.

Immediately after Adam named his wife Eve, God made clothing for Adam and Eve out of animal skins. He provided coverings for their guilt and shame. Remember, Adam and his wife were naked and trying to cover themselves with a poor excuse for a loincloth. Have you ever worn leaves? They don't cover very well. God, who sees all—inside and out—provided genuine leather garments; He covered them with real clothes.

A small act of faith on Adam's part was rewarded with provision from God. This pattern of man's faith followed by God's provision will appear many times in God's story. Let's watch for this and for the Deliverer as His story unfolds.

---

2 The early part of the Bible is written in Hebrew.

After Adam and Eve attempted to cover their guilt and shame with fig leaves, God graciously replaced the leaves with clothing He made from animal skins.

Banishment from the Garden

An oncologist (cancer doctor) knows about cancer intellectually. My friend, Elisabeth, knows about cancer experientially. We are all thankful for doctors who know about cancer, its treatments, and possible cures. But there is a big difference between knowing about cancer and experiencing the pain and anguish of cancer as it destroys your body. Like the doctor, God knew all about sin and the evil effects it would have on humans. When Adam and Eve disobeyed, they experienced sin and its effects.

After God provided coverings for Adam and Eve, He said, "Behold, the man has become like Us in the sense that he knows good and evil now. And he could keep eating from the Tree of Life and live forever—" The fact is that holy, sinless God knows about sin intellectually—not experientially, while Adam and Eve knew evil by personal experience and were contaminated by it. Their fall from innocence would now drastically affect their quality of life. God did not want Adam and Eve to live forever in their new sinful state. Knowing that, God did something that was at the same time an act of judgment and an act of mercy: He drove them out of the garden. Then He set angels as guards with a flaming, flashing sword to the east of the garden. God didn't want man to eat from the Tree of Life and live forever in this sinful state.

Satan had spoken a half-truth when he told Eve she would be like God. When Adam and Eve disobeyed and their eyes were opened, they became more like God in that they knew the difference between good and evil. But they actually became less like God because they had experienced evil which permanently tainted their nature. God is holy and has never sinned. They were created innocent and had not sinned. Now that was over. Now they were sinners.

So God sent Adam out of the garden to cultivate the land from which he had come and set a guard so that living forever in sin could not be an option.

Because Adam and Eve's disobedience caused them to forfeit their privilege to live in the paradise garden where God placed them, He drove them out of it.

Cain and Abel

After a while Adam and Eve had a baby. Eve said, "God has given me a son! I'll call him 'Cain' because with God's help I have acquired a son." (Cain sounds like the Hebrew word for acquire.) She knew God had promised that with a descendant of hers God would judge Satan, so she was happy and probably wondered, "Could this be the one?" Later she gave birth to another son whom she named Abel.

As the boys grew up, Abel became a sheep farmer while Cain worked the soil and raised fruits and vegetables. One day Cain brought some of his harvest as a tribute to the Lord God. Abel also brought a gift; he killed the best of the firstborn lambs of his flock and offered the fat portions. God approved of Abel and his gift, but He did not approve of Cain and his gift. This made Cain very angry, and he could not hide his feelings.

God said to Cain, "Why this tantrum? Why are you walking around with such a sullen look on your face? When you do what you know to be right, won't I accept you? But if you don't do what is right, sin[3] is crouching at the door ready to pounce. Sin is out to get you, but you must master it."

Later Cain invited his brother, Abel, to go for a walk. When they were out in the field, Cain attacked Abel and killed him.

Then God asked Cain, "Where is your brother?"

"How should I know? Am I supposed to take care of my brother—am I his babysitter?"

God replied, "What have you done? I'll tell you: you have killed your brother, and now his blood that poured out on the ground is crying out to Me. Now because you have done this, you are cursed and banished from the ground which soaked up Abel's blood. No matter how hard you work the ground, it will no longer give you good crops. You will be a homeless wanderer on this earth all your life."

---

3 This is the first appearance of the word "sin" in the Bible. It refers to an offense or wronging of someone.

Cain and Abel, the first two sons to be born to Adam and Eve, responded to God in very different ways—Abel in faith and Cain in defiance.

OLD
TESTAMENT

CREATION

FALL

FLOOD

BABEL

PATRIARCHS

MOSES

JOSHUA

JUDGES

MONARCHY

DIVISION

EXILE

RETURN

Seth and His Descendants

When Cain was born, Adam and Eve may have thought he would be God's promised deliverer. As Cain and Abel grew up, Adam and Eve observed their attitudes and behavior before God and may have begun to place their hope in Abel as the promised one. When Cain killed his brother, they must have been deeply disappointed not only in Cain, but also in the realization that the son they thought was the promised one was no more.

Then they had another baby boy. Eve named him Seth, and said, "God has given me a son in the place of Abel." (Seth in this context means "substitute.") How excited Adam and Eve must have been to have another son. God was keeping His promise. They had many other sons and daughters, too, and when Seth grew up, he had a son whom he named Enosh. It was during Enosh's lifetime that men and women began to worship God together.

Sometimes people say the stories in the Bible are just myths— that these events weren't a part of history. But God has given us many indications that the Bible is true. One indication is the genealogies He recorded for us in the Bible. By studying genealogies, we see that the Bible characters were real historical people who lived on this earth, had families, and died. Here is one example of a genealogy in the Bible.

God created humankind as man and woman to be like Himself and blessed them. After the man Adam had lived 130 years, he had a son who was just like him, whom he named Seth. After Seth was born, Adam had many other sons and daughters and lived 800 years. Then he died. After Seth lived for 105 years, he had a son whom he named Enosh.

The genealogy goes on and on, telling how long each person lived, who his most prominent son was, and when he died. This genealogy in Genesis 5 takes us all the way to Noah. His father named him Noah (which means "rest") because he believed that somehow his son, Noah, would bring comfort from the pain and labor that the cursed ground had brought them all those years. He may have been wrong about the relief Noah would bring, but he did have hope that God would do something special through Noah. And He did.

Abel's life ended tragically when his brother, Cain, murdered him, but God gave Adam and Eve a replacement son, Seth, who would become the ancestor of some great godly men.

The Great Flood

As time passed, men and women did so much evil that people were thinking sinister, destructive thoughts and committing violent acts all day and every day. God was grieved by this and knew He must destroy mankind from the face of the earth. But there was one man who found favor in God's eyes; he was so righteous that other men and women couldn't find anything wrong with him. His name was Noah. Noah walked with God.

God had a plan. He would flood the earth and wipe out every living creature on it. But He wanted to save Noah and his family and many species of animals. So He gave Noah the exact instructions he needed to make a boat large enough to carry at least two of every kind of animal on the earth.[4] That's a big boat!

Then God said to Noah, "I will bring floodwaters on the earth to destroy all life under the heavens. Everything will die. But I will make a covenant with you. You and your family will enter the boat with at least two of all the animal kinds (male and female), and I will keep them alive with you. Take food on the boat as well for you and for the animals."

So Noah built the boat and the day came that God said to him, "Go into the boat with your family." Then God brought animals to Noah from all over the earth, and God shut them in. (Notice: as with judgment so with salvation, God takes the initiative.)

Then deep springs burst up from the ground, and the floodgates of heaven opened and poured down. The rain kept coming for 40 days so that the water rose higher and higher and lifted the boat up and up. The water rose so much that the highest mountains on earth were covered.

Well, just as God said, every living creature on the earth died—except for Noah, his family, and the animals on Noah's boat. Then the water receded steadily so that after five months the water was low enough for the boat to rest on the mountains of Ararat. When the earth was completely dry, God told Noah to come out of the boat with his family and the animals so they could multiply and fill the earth again.

Then Noah built an altar to God and sacrificed burnt offerings. God saw Noah's worship, smelled the pleasing aroma, and said in his heart, "Never again will I curse the ground for the sinful things its people do even though the imagination of their heart is wicked from childhood. Never again will I destroy all living creatures."

So Noah and his wife, their sons, Shem, Ham, and Japheth, and their wives came out of the great boat. From them came people who scattered over the earth.

---

4 Noah's boat, with a capacity of about 40,000 cubic meters (equal to about 1,500 semi-trailers!), was the largest floating vessel ever until the mid-nineteenth century. It could easily carry the required load, and its width and height ratios made it stable.

Throughout the years to follow, the human race grew and became so sinful that God destroyed the earth and its inhabitants with a great flood, except for God-fearing Noah and his family.

The Tower of Babel

Now Noah was not perfect; neither were Adam and Eve, Abel, or Seth. But they did acknowledge the Lord God of the Bible as the one true living God who created heaven and earth and all that is therein. They came to know Him as a loving, merciful God who is also righteous and holy in His dealings with people. They also recognized His unlimited power and self-dependency.

But self-centered people began to re-create God into someone with whom they were more comfortable. They said, "God is powerful, but He has weaknesses, too. Besides, He is needy and only we can meet His needs."

Then, "Since God is weak, maybe there are many gods, each making up for others' weaknesses."

"These weak gods don't always communicate clearly. If we don't pamper the gods, then they will become hostile and threaten to hurt us."

Eventually, the majority of people believed that the gods could be manipulated by humans. Things deteriorated so that they worshiped many gods instead of the true, living God.

One day, in the plain of Shinar, many who had settled there decided to build a huge tower out of brick and mortar. They said to each other, "Come on, let's build a city and a tower that reaches up to heaven. We will be famous and won't be scattered all over the earth."

So, even though God had said to fill the earth, the majority of the people chose to do the opposite of God's commandment. They began to build a city with a tower that went high into the sky and called this tower the gateway to the gods, reaching up to their home. They imagined gods coming down the long stairways to the temple at the bottom of the tower to be appeased and interact with the priests and priestesses.

So God "came down" to see the city and the tower men were building. He said, "Look, they are all staying together and are united in their disobedience, since they speak the same language. Something has to be done or they will continue in this folly. Let's go down and break them up, by making them speak different languages so they won't be able to understand each other."

You can imagine the confusion. One man asks for a tool, another doesn't understand. Fights may even have broken out. The work on the city definitely stopped because God confused their language and scattered them all over the earth.

The Babylonian name of their city literally meant "gateway of the gods." "Babel" is the Hebrew translation of that name which sounds like the Hebrew word for confusion. Both ideas convey the story of the tower of Babel.

Several generations later, the descendants of Noah assembled together to build a stairway tower as a "gateway of the gods," but the LORD God confused their language and scattered them.

Promises to Abram

After Babel, man continued to degrade (de-God) God to such an extent that before long people were worshiping animals and inanimate objects such as the sun, moon, and stars. Mesopotamia (west of modern-day Iran, in eastern Turkey) had two significant centers of moon worship: Ur and Haran. Ur, located near where the Euphrates and Tigris flow into the Persian Gulf, was a highly cultured and influential city with a large ziggurat (Babel-like tower) dominating its landscape.

Terah, a moon-worshiper living in Ur, had three sons: Abram, Nahor, and Haran. They each married and stayed close to home. Haran's wife had a son whom they named Lot. How pleased Terah must have been to have a grandson! But Sarai, Abram's wife, was unable to have children. Then a worse tragedy struck: Haran died, leaving his son without a father. Terah took his grandson, Lot, into his home.

Then one day, Terah decided to leave Ur. He took his son Abram, his daughter-in-law Sarai, and his grandson, Lot, with him as he traveled north along the river to Haran before he settled down. That's where Terah died, a dedicated old moon-worshiper.

How long would this continue? Would man never turn back to the living God who created him?

God initiated contact with a single man. God spoke to Abram! "I want you to leave your country, your people, and your family and go to a land I will show you. I will make you a great nation, and I will bless you; I will make you famous and through you I'll bless others. Yes, I will bless anyone who blesses you and curse anyone who curses you. Yet all families of the earth will be blessed through you."

So Abram did as God said; he left. At age seventy-five, he took his wife, his nephew, Lot, and all the possessions and people he had accumulated in Haran and went down to Canaan.

Abram arrived in Shechem, where the Canaanites lived. These people worshiped a pantheon of gods, some human in form, others half-human, half-animal, almost all related to fertility. There God appeared to Abram again. "To your children I will give this land." So Abram built an altar to God right there to show his allegiance to the true and living God despite the fact his own wife was still infertile.

Then Abram moved farther south to a place later called Bethel. He settled there, built another altar to God, and worshiped Him.

Abram, his father, and his people were moon-worshipers. In Canaan, people were worshiping all kinds of false gods. Yet once again God graciously communicated to someone undeserving. Abram is now a light of hope in a dark world—a lone man following the true God in a world of counterfeit gods.

Sometime after the tower of Babel incident, God called Abram to be the father of a great nation through which all families of the earth would receive a special blessing.

Destruction of Sodom

God blessed Abram and his family so much that he and his nephew, Lot, couldn't stay together. Their flocks and herds and possessions were too much for one place! So Abram told Lot to choose where he wanted to live, and whichever direction Lot went, Abram would go the other way.

Lot took a look around. He saw that the plain of the Jordan Valley was well watered—almost like the Garden of Eden—and as beautiful as Egypt. He chose that valley and headed east with his flocks and servants. So Abram settled in Canaan while Lot moved his tents near Sodom. The people of Sodom were wicked, continually sinning against the Lord.

Later, Lot moved right into the city. Then two angels arrived at Sodom one evening while Lot was sitting at the city gate. He got up to welcome them. Bowing, he said, "Please come stay the night at my house. Wash up. You can rise early and be on your way refreshed."

They said, "No, we'll sleep in the street." But he wouldn't take no for an answer; so they relented and went with him. Lot fixed a hot meal for them, and they ate.

Before they went to bed, men from all over Sodom, young and old, surrounded the house. They yelled, "Where are your visitors? Send them out so that we can have sex with them!"

Lot went outside, shut the door behind him, and said, "Friends, please don't do such a terrible thing! I have two single daughters. I'll bring them out, and you can have your pleasure with them. But don't harm these men. They are guests in my home."

"Get out of here! You're an outsider; and now you're going to tell us what we can and can't do? We'll do worse things to you than we're going to do to them!" They rushed Lot to break down the door. But the two angels reached out and pulled Lot safely inside. Then they struck the crowd blind, leaving them confused, groping in the dark.

The two men said to Lot, "The terrible things done in this city are rising up to God. He sent us to destroy this wicked place. If you have any family here, get them out—fast!"

Lot went out to warn his daughters' fiancés, "Hurry, get out of the city; God is about to destroy it!" But they just laughed at him.

At daybreak the angels pushed Lot to get a move on. "Hurry! Get your wife and daughters out of here before it's too late and you're caught in the judgment of the city."

Lot just stood there! But because God wanted to save his family, the men grabbed their arms and led them to safety outside the city. Then, one said, "Now run for your lives! Don't look back! Don't stop anywhere in the valley—run for the hills, or you'll be swept away."

The sun was high in the sky when Lot arrived at Zoar. Then God rained brimstone and fire down on Sodom and Gomorrah—a river of lava from God out of the sky! He destroyed the cities, the entire plain, everyone who lived in the cities, and all the vegetation. But Lot's wife turned to go back. In an instant she became a pillar of salt.

Abram got up early the next morning and went to the place where he had recently stood with God. He looked down toward Sodom and Gomorrah and saw smoke rising from all over the land—it was like a flaming furnace.

And that's the story of the destruction of Sodom and Gomorrah, the valley where Lot lived. However, God, who is just, holy, merciful, and slow to get angry, remembered a promise He made to Abram and got Lot out of there before He blasted those cities off the face of the earth.

The city of Sodom was exceedingly sinful, so the LORD God destroyed it with a rain of fiery sulphur, but He saved Abram's nephew Lot and Lot's daughters from harm.

Abram's Son Ishmael

About 10 years passed since God promised Abram he would have a son. I imagine he began to wonder if it would ever happen. Could God's Word be trusted?

God spoke to Abram again. "Don't you worry, Abram. I, your God and King, will care for you and reward you abundantly."

Abram responded, "Master, You have given me all I could ever want … except for a son. When I die, my servant will receive all my wealth because You have given me no children."

"Oh no, he won't," God answered. "You will have a son of your very own, and he will receive everything you have. Look up at the stars. Count them if you can. That's how many descendants will come from you!"

Abram believed God, and God considered him in right standing with Himself.

What Abram had suggested about his servant being his heir was not wrong. In fact, it was quite common for the servant of a childless couple to become the heir. Another common practice for a barren wife was to give her handmaiden to her husband so that he could have children through the servant. That's probably why Sarai told Abram to take her Egyptian maid, Hagar, and try to have a baby with her. These practices were accepted in the culture, but it was not God's plan to fulfill His promises of blessing and land for Abram and Sarai.

However, Abram listened to his wife and had intercourse with Hagar, who became pregnant. This created strife between the two women, Sarai mistreated her, and Hagar ran away.

But God saw Hagar in the desert, heard her cry, and sent an angel to encourage her. The angel said, "Go back to Sarai and humbly submit to her, and I will bless your descendants abundantly. Listen, the baby growing inside you is a boy. I want you to name him Ishmael (God hears) because God hears and cares about you. Ishmael and his descendants will be like a wild donkey, always roaming and contrary, living to the east of their relatives."

Hagar called that spring Beer-lahai-roi (A Well to the Living One Who Sees Me), realizing God had seen her affliction. Then she went back to Abram and Sarai.

When Abram was 86 years old, Hagar's son was born. Abram gave him the name Ishmael.

Several years later, God told Abram again that he would have a son, and God changed his name from Abram (Revered Father) to Abraham (Father of Many Nations). Then God said, "Abraham, your wife's name will now be Sarah. I will bless her; she will have a son, and some of her descendants will even be kings."

Abraham fell on his face and laughed! "How could I, a man soon to be 100, and Sarah, an old woman of 90, have a son? Why not just let Ishmael be my heir?"

"No! You and Sarah will have a son; his name will be Isaac (Laughter), and my everlasting promise will pass to him and his descendants. As for Ishmael, I have heard you and will bless him; he will be the father of 12 princes, and his family will become a great nation. But your son Isaac will be born about this time next year, and My promise to you and your family will be for him and his descendants forever."

Abram believed God would provide a son for him, but his wife, Sarai, could not bear children so she devised her own plan to make that happen through her handmaiden.

Abraham's Son Isaac

A year later when Abraham was 100 and Sarah was 90 years old, their miracle baby was born. How excited they must have been! I'm sure they had great times bringing up their boy.

A few years later God put Abraham through a test. "Abraham!" He called.

"Here I am."

"Take your son, your only son, Isaac, whom you love, and go to Moriah. I want you to sacrifice him as a burnt offering to Me there on a mountain I will show you."

Wow! What a difficult request! The Bible tells us Abraham obeyed immediately by starting on the journey the next morning. But he must have thought about it all night. In fact, another book in the Bible tells how Abraham reasoned that "God could raise the dead." Maybe such reasoning was a little comfort to him, but this still would be a difficult task.

Early the next morning Abraham got up, saddled the donkey, got two servants, and his son Isaac. He chopped wood for the burnt offering, and they started on their way to the place God had told him about. On the third day Abraham looked up and saw the place. He turned to his servants. "Wait here with the donkey. I and the boy will go on. We will worship and we will return to you."

Then he arranged the wood on Isaac's back, but he carried the hot coals and the knife as they set off together for the mountain God had shown him. As they walked, Isaac said, "Father?"

Abraham answered, "Here I am."

Isaac said, "I have the wood here, and I see you have the knife and the coals … but where is the lamb for the burnt offering?"

"God Himself will provide a lamb for the offering." And the two of them went on together.

When they reached the indicated place, they stopped. Abraham gathered stones, built an altar, and arranged the wood on the altar. Then he tied up his son and laid him on the altar. He unsheathed his knife.

"Abraham! Abraham!"

"Here I am."

"Don't harm the boy. Now I know that you fear God because you have not kept back your son, your only son."

Abraham looked up and saw a ram caught in a bush by its horns. He took the ram and sacrificed it as a burnt offering to the Lord in the place of his son. Then he called the place "The Lord will provide."

The angel of the Lord called to him again. "The Lord said, 'I swear by myself, because you have not withheld your only son, beyond a doubt I will make your descendants as numerous as the stars in the sky and the sand on the beach. Your descendant will rule over his enemies, and through him I will bless all the nations.'"

After they worshiped together, Abraham and Isaac went down the mountain, met the servants with the donkey, and went home.

God later gave Abraham a special son through his wife, Sarah, but then tested Abraham's faith by telling him to offer Isaac back to Himself.

Isaac's Son Jacob

Isaac grew up and married a beautiful woman named Rebekah. But Rebekah couldn't have children. So Isaac prayed to God for his wife, and she became pregnant! And that's not all; God spoke to Rebekah.

Two nations are inside your womb,
Two peoples will come out of you.
Yes, one people will be stronger,
The older will serve the younger.

Rebekah's first son was born with a full head of hair, so they named him Esau (hairy). When his twin brother was born, his hand grabbed on to Esau's heel, so he was named Jacob (trickster). This was a foretaste of trouble between these brothers.

One day Jacob tricked Esau out of his inheritance. With the help of his mother, Jacob then deceived his father into giving him Esau's special blessing which would make him the head of the family when Isaac died. Esau was not happy at all with that and planned to kill Jacob as soon as his father died. Once again mother and son planned a trick that would keep Jacob safe. Rebekah told Isaac that she didn't want Jacob to marry a woman from Canaan; instead he should go back to her homeland to find a wife.

It worked. Isaac called for Jacob. When he came in, Isaac said, "Jacob, I don't want you to marry a Canaanite woman. Go back to Paddan Aram where your mother used to live and find a wife there. May God bless you with many children and possessions and may He give your descendants the land He promised to Abraham."

So Jacob started on the 500-mile journey that would take him to his mother's homeland. When it got dark, he stopped for the night, lay down, and fell fast asleep. In a dream he saw a huge stairway from the ground to the heavens with angels going up and down on it. God was standing at the top and spoke to him.

"I am YHWH, the God of your grandfather, Abraham, and your father, Isaac. I will give you and your descendants the land on which you are lying. Your descendants will be like dust—too many to count and scattered all over the earth. All of the peoples of the earth will be blessed through a descendant of yours."

When Jacob woke up, he realized the importance of his encounter with God. He called that place Bethel (House of God).

He went on his way and reached the home of his mother's family. He found a wife and became very wealthy. But his father-in-law's deceptive ways brought him trouble. Finally, he left that area and headed back to Canaan, fearing for his life.

On his way home he had another divine encounter; he wrestled with an angel from God all through the night. He wouldn't give in even though the angel wounded his hip badly. He continued to hang on, asking for a blessing. The angel asked him his name, to which he replied, "Jacob" (trickster or deceiver).

Then the angel said, "Not anymore. From now on your name is Israel (wrestles with God or God wrestles) because you have wrestled with God and men and come through." How exciting to be blessed with a new name!

Isaac's son Jacob was a deceitful man whose life God changed and who became the recipient of the promises God had given to Abraham and Isaac.

Israel's Family to Egypt

Israel (formerly Jacob) had many sons and daughters whom he loved, but Joseph (the eleventh son) held a special place in his heart because he was the son of his old age. His brothers noticed the special treatment Joseph received and hated him for it. One day they ripped his special robe off that he had received from his father and threw him into a cistern. Then they sold him for 20 pieces of silver to some merchants (descendants of Ishmael) that came by, taking him to Egypt.

The merchants sold Joseph to Potiphar, Pharaoh's captain of the guard. God blessed Joseph; so much so that his master Potiphar noticed. Potiphar was convinced that Joseph's success was the result of God being with him, and he promoted him.

Later, Joseph was falsely accused and sent to prison, but God continued to bless him. Even in prison he was given great responsibility. When Joseph was released, God revealed a plan to Joseph that would save Egypt from great famine. When Joseph revealed that plan to Pharaoh, he said, "I name you governor of all Egypt!"

When the severe famine came to all the countries, only Egypt had food. All the nations came to Egypt to buy grain from Joseph. Just like the others, Israel heard that there was food available in Egypt, so he sent his sons (Joseph's brothers) down to Egypt to buy food. They thought Joseph had died and did not recognize that this important leader was their brother.

Joseph tested them to see if they were repentant of the terrible thing they had done to him. He arranged to send his brothers home, leaving behind their youngest brother, Benjamin, as a slave.

Judah led the way in pleading with Joseph not to do such a thing, offering himself as a slave in Benjamin's place.

Joseph saw they were repentant and said, "Come close. Look. Yes, it is me, your brother Joseph, whom you sold as a slave!" The brothers were aghast. Joseph said, "Don't worry or be angry with yourselves because God sent me here ahead of you to save lives—especially to preserve our family. Go get Father and hurry back down here!"

On the way down to see Joseph, Israel offered sacrifices, and God spoke to him in a vision, saying, "I am God, the God of your father. Don't be afraid to go to Egypt because I will make you into a great nation there. I will go down to Egypt with you, and I will certainly bring you back again."

That is how Israel and his family ended up in Egypt for many years. Pharaoh gave some of the best land to Joseph for his father and brothers: Goshen. Before he died, Israel called all his sons together and blessed each one, predicting what would happen in the future. He gave a special prediction blessing to Judah.

It's you, Judah, that your brothers will praise;
Upon you they'll gaze as the scepter you raise.
You'll rule over all—brothers and enemies—
As all bend their knees and everyone sees
That all power is yours; it will never depart
From you, and all nations obey from the heart.

God directed events in Israel's family to place his son Joseph as a prominent leader in Egypt for a critical time in the early history of this very important family.

Israelites in Egypt

When Israel moved to Egypt, he brought with him all his other sons (Reuben, Simeon, Levi, Judah, Issachar, Zebulun, Benjamin, Dan, Naphtali, Gad, and Asher) and their families—70 people in all. In the course of time, Joseph, his brothers, and all that generation died, but God continued to bless the Israelites. They became so numerous that they filled the land of Goshen.

Living in Egypt meant they were surrounded by counterfeit gods again. The Egyptians worshiped 1,500 different gods who were not creators but were considered to be forces within nature. Some were part human, some part animal, and some were other entities such as the Nile River. But they all had one thing in common: they were all going to die one day. Pharaoh was also considered a god—partial while living, but becoming fully god when he died.

The Egyptians created statues (idols) in which the gods could reside. They also built temples as houses for them. Instead of God caring for people, people took care of the gods. In fact, the role of the priests was to keep the gods and goddesses happy. How different from the God of the Bible!

The Egyptian belief about creation tells the story of their principal god. Long ago before anyone lived on the earth, an eternal, infinite, lifeless ocean existed. Then a pyramidal mound of ground emerged from the ocean, and then the sun god (Ra) appeared. Now he races across the sky every day.

The Egyptians placed great importance on the sun, while many Mesopotamians worshiped the moon. Interesting, when one considers that when God created the sun and the moon, he didn't even name them!

After about one hundred years passed since Joseph and Israel moved to Egypt, the Israelites continued to multiply. A new king came to power who did not realize all Joseph had done for Egypt. He said to his people, "The Israelites are becoming too numerous and are becoming more powerful than we. If we are not careful, they will grow even larger and join our enemies to fight against us and leave the country. Then we won't have cheap labor anymore! We must outsmart them."

So the Egyptians put slave bosses over them to wear them down with hard labor. They forced them to build two store cities for Pharaoh: Pithom and Rameses.

But the more the Israelites were oppressed, the more they multiplied and spread. The Egyptians became even more concerned, so they made their lives miserable through more work and cruel punishment. Then Pharaoh began killing all the baby boys, insisting they be thrown in the Nile.

Life in Egypt became nearly unbearable for the Israelites. They cried out to God, begging for help.

In spite of intense oppression by a new king of Egypt who did not know about Joseph, God blessed the Israelites and they multiplied greatly in Egypt.

Moses' Call to Leadership

One of those Israelite babies was not thrown into the Nile. After putting him in a basket, his mother set it afloat in the Nile, trusting God to protect him. Pharaoh's daughter found the boy and reared him, naming him Moses. Ironically, one of the boys Pharaoh wanted dead grew up in his own home.

After Moses became a man, he killed an Egyptian whom he had seen beating a Hebrew (one of his people). He fled Egypt and became a shepherd in the wilderness of Sinai for 40 years.

One day, as he led his flock near Mount Horeb, he saw a bush all ablaze that wasn't consumed by the fire. He thought it unusual, so he approached the bush.

"Moses! Moses!" God called from the bush.

"Here I am," Moses answered.

"Stay where you are. Take off your sandals. You are standing on holy ground. I am the God your ancestors Abraham, Isaac, and Jacob worshiped."

Moses, afraid to look at God, shed his shoes and covered his face. God continued to speak.

"I have seen the misery and oppression of my people in Egypt. I have heard them beg for help and have come down to rescue them. I will deliver them out of Egypt and give them the fruitful land of the Canaanites. So go to Pharaoh. I am sending you to bring my people, the Israelites, out of Egypt."

But Moses said to God, "I am nobody special. How can I go to Pharaoh?"

"How? I will be with you! You will know that I am the One who sent you when you worship me again on this mountain after you lead my people out of Egypt."

Moses asked another question: "If I go to the Israelites in that land of many gods and say, 'The God of your ancestors has sent me,' they might ask me your name. What should I say?"

"I am the eternal God, the self-existent One. Tell the Israelites 'I Am' has sent you. This is my eternal name and the name by which I will be remembered. Bring the leaders together and tell them that the LORD, the God of your ancestors, appeared to you and said, 'I have seen your trouble. I promise to deliver you and bring you to the land of the Canaanites.'"

Moses asked a third question: "What if they don't believe me or say, 'God didn't appear to you'?"

God asked, "What's in your hand?"

Moses replied, "A walking stick."

"Throw it down."

Moses threw it on the ground. Immediately it became a snake, and Moses jumped away.

"Pick it up by its tail." When Moses did, it turned right back into his walking stick.

"Do this so they will believe that the God of their ancestors Abraham, Isaac, and Jacob has sent you."

Moses went back to Egypt, and with his brother Aaron, called a meeting of the Israelite leaders. They told the leaders what God said to Moses and performed the miracle. The Israelites believed and worshiped God because they knew He had seen their suffering and was going to deliver them.

God called Moses to lead the Israelites out of Egypt and into the land of Canaan, the place God earlier promised to Abraham.

Plagues in Egypt

When 80-year-old Moses walked into 20-year-old Pharaoh Amenhotep's throne room to challenge him to let the Israelites go, they couldn't have been more different. Moses was old and maybe a bit weary from chasing sheep around the desert. Pharaoh was a well-developed hunter and outdoorsman in his prime and ready to take on anything life would throw at him—or so he thought.

Yet the contest wasn't between these two, but between the LORD God and the supposed gods of Egypt (including Pharaoh himself who was thought to be a god).

Moses told Pharaoh, "The LORD God wants you to let His people go to worship Him in the desert."

Pharaoh responded, "Who is this LORD God that I should obey Him? Forget it!" He even made their work harder as punishment. Moses did the walking stick/snake miracle, but Pharaoh stubbornly refused to let the people go.

So God told Moses to take his walking stick and warn Pharaoh that if he didn't let them go, he would strike the Nile River—one of Egypt's gods—and turn it to blood. It would stink. Fish would die. People would get sick. Moses warned Pharaoh, but he didn't listen. So Moses struck the river, and it all happened as God had said it would, demonstrating God's authority over Hapy, god of the Nile, over Osiris, god of vegetation (Nile was his bloodstream), and over Hatmehyt, the fish goddess. This became a pattern.

Moses insisted that the people be freed and warned of another plague. Pharaoh refused. God brought the plague through Moses, each time showing His power over the counterfeit gods.

After the Nile debacle, God afflicted the Egyptians with frogs—everywhere! God showed He could bring frogs and take them away, demonstrating victory over Heket, the frog-headed goddess of birth.

Then came gnats—as thick as dust. Then swarms of flies ruined the land. Then God sent a plague on all the livestock of the Egyptians and boils on the people and animals. God sent hail and lightning, ruining all the fields. Then so many locusts came such as had never been seen before or would be seen again. Each time God was showing His superiority over the counterfeit gods of Egypt.

Finally, Moses stretched out his hand toward the sky, and God sent total darkness over all Egypt for three days. No one could move. Ra, the sun god, was defeated.

This time, Pharaoh called for Moses and said, "Go worship the LORD! Take your families but leave your sheep and cattle."

"No!" Moses replied. "We must take our animals to sacrifice to the LORD our God."

Pharaoh was stubborn. He yelled, "Get out and stay out! I never want to see you again!"

Moses responded, "Have it your way. You won't see me again."

In order to convince Pharaoh, the king of Egypt, to release the Israelites from their bondage, God used Moses to afflict Egypt with some dreadful plagues.

The Passover

God told Moses about one more plague He would bring on the Egyptians, so before Moses left Pharaoh's presence for the last time, he said, "Here is God's message."

"At midnight I will pass through Egypt, and every firstborn will die—from Pharaoh's firstborn who sits on the throne to the firstborn of the poorest slave girl. The firstborn of cattle will also die. What loud lamentation there will be all over Egypt! And yet, no one will offer the least resistance to Israel when they leave. In fact, your officials will get on their knees and beg them to leave. This is to show you the distinction I make between Egypt and Israel."

Osiris, an important, revered god of Egypt, was the fearsome god of death and the underworld. Because he was the god of the underworld, he was also the god of vegetation. With this plague, the LORD God was about to demonstrate that He alone is the true God of life and death.

God had a related but different message for the Israelites. He told Moses: "Tell the whole community of Israel that on the tenth day of the month each family must choose a one-year-old, healthy male lamb without defect. They will take care of it until the fourteenth day of the month when they will slaughter the lamb at twilight. Then, they will dip a bunch of hyssop in the blood, and they must spread the blood on both sides of the frame and the top of the doorframe of the house in which they will eat the lamb. And here is how they are to eat it: roast the meat with fire and eat it with bitter herbs and bread made without yeast, and be dressed to travel with staff in hand. Eat it quickly. This is the LORD's Passover. On that night I will pass through Egypt and strike down every firstborn and bring judgment on all the gods of Egypt. I am the LORD. When I see the blood on the doorframes, I will pass over you. Nothing will happen to you when I strike Egypt."

So Moses assembled all the leaders of Israel and gave them this message. Then the people bowed down, worshiped God, and went out to do exactly as He commanded.

Then it happened. At midnight the LORD struck every firstborn in Egypt. Pharaoh, his officials—everyone in Egypt—got up and cried bitterly because there was not one home where someone had not died. But the Israelites who expressed faith in God by obeying His word were safe. Their firstborn sons didn't die.

Pharaoh called for Moses and Aaron and said, "Up and out! Leave us, all of you Israelites! Take your flocks and herds and go worship the LORD as you asked. Just go. But ask God to be kind to me."

God sent a final plague upon Egypt, which resulted in the death of firstborn sons, but God protected those families who appropriately expressed faith in Him.

The Exodus from Egypt

Four hundred thirty years after Israel and his family moved to Egypt, the LORD led them—now a nation of two million—along with others and their livestock, out of Egypt. They walked from Rameses to Succoth.

But when Pharaoh and his officials realized Israel had left, they said, "What have we done? We let our slave labor go free!" So Pharaoh prepared his army with all its chariots and chased after the Israelites.

When the Israelites saw Pharaoh and his army marching after them, they were terrified and cried out to God. They whined to Moses, "Weren't the cemeteries in Egypt large enough that you had to bring us out in the wilderness to die? Why did you do this? We would rather be slaves in Egypt than to die out here."

Moses answered the people, "Don't be afraid. Hang on and you will see the LORD deliver you in such a way that you will never see these Egyptians again. The LORD will do the fighting; you won't have to do a thing."

Then the LORD said to Moses, "Get the people moving. Hold your walking stick up over the sea and divide it. The Israelites will walk right through the sea on dry ground. Meanwhile, I will make Pharaoh and his army stubborn in the chase so that they come in after you. The Egyptians will know that I am the LORD when I use their army, chariots, and horsemen to glorify Myself."

The angel of almighty God had been leading the Israelites. He now went behind them, taking the pillar of cloud with him. Now the cloud was between the Egyptians and the Israelites, bringing darkness to the Egyptians and light to the Israelites and separating them throughout the night.

Then Moses lifted his walking stick over the sea, and God, with a thunderous east wind, drove the sea back. The sea split in two, leaving dry ground in the middle. The Israelites walked through the sea on dry ground with a wall of water on each side.

The Egyptians went in after them. God looked down through the pillar and brought them into confusion. He clogged up the chariot wheels. The Egyptians began to shout, "Run from Israel! The LORD is fighting for them against us!"

On the other side, God told Moses, "Stretch your walking stick out over the sea so that the water will flow back over the Egyptian army." Moses obeyed, the sea returned, and the LORD swept them into it. Not one of the army that pursued Israel into the sea survived. History shows that for several years after this, the Egyptian army did not go out to show its power; its power was so greatly diminished on that day.

But the Israelites had passed through the sea on dry ground. The LORD delivered Israel from the oppression of Egypt that day, leaving Egyptians to wash up dead on the shore. When the Israelites observed the tremendous power of the LORD, they gained a healthy, holy respect for Him and trusted in Him and His servant Moses.

Then Moses led the Israelites out of Egypt as God parted the waters of the Red Sea, preparing their way toward the promised land of Canaan.

The Mosaic Covenant

Three months later, the Israelites arrived in the Desert of Sinai and set up camp facing Mount Sinai (Horeb). Moses went up the mountain, and God spoke to him again.

"Tell Israel: You saw with your own eyes what I did to Egypt and how I brought you to Myself as a mighty eagle carries its young. Now if you will obey My voice and keep My covenant, I will make you My treasured possession. The entire earth and its nations are mine, but you will be a kingdom of priests for me and a holy nation."

So Moses went back and told the leaders what God had said. The people responded as one: "Everything God says we will do."

So God told Moses, "Get the people ready. Tell them to wash up and prepare themselves for two days. I will come down to the mountain to make My presence known. Have them stay back. No one is to approach the mountain, or they will die."

On the third day came deafening thunder, lightning, smoke all around the mountain, and a loud trumpet blast. The people trembled with fear. The mountain was all in smoke and quaked violently because God descended on it as fire. Then God spoke to Moses, establishing His covenant with Israel. He said, "I am the LORD your God who brought you out of bondage in Egypt."

As part of the covenant, He gave them an extensive system of laws. The core of this moral and legal system is what is often called the Ten Commandments.

"Do not worship any god except Me."

"Do not make idols that look like anything in the sky or on the earth or in the waters. Do not bow down to or worship idols."

"Do not misuse My name. I am the LORD your God and will punish anyone who does."

"Do not work on the seventh day of the week. That day is mine. Keep it separate; treat it differently."

"Respect your father and mother, and you will live a long time in the land I am giving you."

"Do not murder."

"Do not commit adultery; be faithful in marriage."

"Do not steal."

"Do not tell lies about others."

"Do not set your heart on anything—spouse, servants, animals, furnishings—anything that belongs to someone else."

In the wilderness between Egypt and Canaan, the holy LORD God made a covenant with Israel and gave them a set of laws which expresses His hatred for what we know as "sin."

The Golden Calf Rebellion

Moses read all the laws to the people, and twice more they declared, "All the LORD has spoken we will do; we will be obedient." The LORD God wanted to live with His people and let His presence be known among them. So He called Moses back up the mountain to give him instructions for building a tabernacle—a structure where God's presence would be, where God could take away their guilt, and where they could worship God.

To the people it seemed like forever that Moses was on the mountain, so they gathered around Aaron and said, "Do something! Make us gods to lead us. We don't know what has happened to Moses."

So Aaron told them to bring him all the gold earrings they had, and he shaped the gold into a calf. Then the people shouted, "These are your gods, O Israel, who brought you up out of Egypt!" Aaron observed this, built an altar, and announced, "Tomorrow we will have a festival to the LORD." So the people got up early the next day and sacrificed burnt offerings. The whole thing turned into a wild, drunken party.

These were the people that declared, "All the LORD has spoken we will do; we will be obedient." They broke the first two commandments in worshiping this bull and who knows what other commandments during the orgy!

God knew what was happening, so He told Moses, "Hurry down the mountain. Those people you brought out of Egypt have corrupted themselves. They have already stopped obeying me and made an idol in the shape of a young bull. They bowed down to it, sacrificed to it, and said, 'These are your gods, Israel!'"

When Moses got close to the camp and saw the bull and the people dancing around, he was furious. He threw the tablets of commandments down, smashing them to smithereens! Then he took the calf, burned it up, ground it to powder, scattered it on the water, and made the Israelites drink it. The next day Moses said to the people, "This thing you have done is a great sin. But I will go up to the LORD to see if I can do something to remove the offense of your sin." Moses attempted to be a mediator between God and the Israelites.

So Moses went to the LORD and cried, "How great is this people's sin! They made gods of gold. Please forgive their sin—but if not, blot me out of the book you have written."

The LORD responded, "Whoever has sinned against me I will blot out of my book. But go, lead the people to the place I told you about; my angel will go before you. But know this, when the time comes I will punish them for their sin."

So the LORD punished the people with a terrible disease for what they did with the idol.

Not long after God delivered the Israelites from slavery in Egypt and gave His laws to them, they rebelled against Him and created a golden image to worship.

Tabernacle in the Wilderness

God still wanted to "tabernacle" (dwell) among His people, so He had Moses tell the people to bring offerings to Him so that they could build a tabernacle according to the pattern He showed Moses. They brought precious metals, gems, colored yarns, fine linen, animal skins, wood, olive oil, spices, and incense.

When all the pieces were made, Moses set up the main structure of the tabernacle, 45 feet by 15 feet, facing east. Then the tent—10 curtains of fine twisted linen and blue, purple, and red yarn—was spread over the frame. The final covering over the tent, made from three types of hides covering linen curtains, was laid over the tent just as God had instructed.

Then Moses put the second set of stones with the Ten Commandments written on them in the ark (a gold-covered box) and placed the mercy seat (a pure gold covering for the ark with a gold angel at either end) on the ark. He took the ark inside the tabernacle and hung the shielding curtain, a veil woven with colorful threads, to separate the Holy Place from the Holy of Holies, a 15- by 15-foot chamber.

With the tent now separated, Moses placed the table and the lampstand inside the tent on the north and south sides, respectively. Both were outside the veil. The table would hold 12 loaves of fresh bread placed on it each Sabbath. The lampstand, a hammered piece of solid pure gold, had a central shaft with six branches to light the Holy Place.

Next, the gold altar was placed inside the Tent of Meeting right in front of the curtain, and Moses began burning incense on it as the LORD had commanded. Then he hung the curtain at the entrance of the Tabernacle, completing the Tent of Meeting.

Outside the tent, directly to the east, Moses set up the altar of burnt offering and began offering burnt offerings and grain offerings on it as the LORD had commanded. The altar was a 7.5- by 7.5-foot by 4.5-foot structure made of wood and covered in bronze. In between the altar and the Tent of Meeting he placed the basin, a bronze laver containing water, so that the priests could wash their hands and feet before and after ministering.

Finally, Moses set up a 150-foot-long and 75-foot-wide courtyard around the Tabernacle and altar surrounded by a 7.5-foot-high fence of linen curtains. At the east end he hung panels of blue, purple, red, and white as the entry curtain.

The Tabernacle and its courtyard were now ready for use. God would meet with His people, and they could have their sins taken out of the way.

Moses built a portable place for worship, a "tabernacle," so that God could dwell with them during their wilderness journey.

OLD
TESTAMENT

CREATION
FALL
FLOOD
BABEL
PATRIARCHS
MOSES
JOSHUA
JUDGES
MONARCHY
DIVISION
EXILE
RETURN

God's Provision for Forgiveness

Ahira Ben-Enan[5] eagerly walked the lamb from the pen to his family's tent. Today was the day his family's sins would be expiated—they would be taken out of the way. He threw open the tent door.

"Come on out! I have the lamb. Let's get over to the Tabernacle."

His dear wife, flashing him a big smile, came out holding their newborn baby girl. Then his firstborn, Enan, emerged yawning and stretching his arms, and finally little Naphtali. Even though "Tali" was the last one out, he had the brightest eyes and seemed the most excited about the sacrifice. As they walked, Tali was full of questions.

"Abba, why does the lamb have to die?"

"Well, Tali, God is holy, and …"

"What's holy?"

"Holy means that God is totally good, without sin. He doesn't do wrong things like we do, and our sins separate us from Him. Our sins have a penalty …"

"What's penalty?"

"Penalty means our sins have to be paid for."

"How much do sins cost?"

"Well, the payment for sin is death. That means we would have to die to pay for our sins. But God loves us so much that He allowed us to offer a substitute to die in our place."

"S-s-susistute? Is that the lamb?"

"That's right. I chose this lamb for our substitute because God said the lamb had to be a male without defect—the best we have."

Others were also walking toward the Tabernacle. Some carried pigeons; one father led a fine-looking young bull. Tali tugged on his father's robe, whispering. "Tell them it's 'posed to be a lamb, Abba."

"Actually, Tali, God wants everyone to come—rich or poor. People can bring an animal from their herd or flock, but if they don't have the means, they can bring a dove or a pigeon."

They arrived at the Tabernacle, and Aaron motioned for Ahira to come through the entrance. His family stood just outside the Tabernacle and watched quietly through the open curtain as Ahira knelt down and placed his hand on the head of the lamb. Then he took his knife and quickly slit the throat of the substitute. One of Aaron's sons caught the blood in a bowl and then sprinkled it on the altar. They watched as the head of their home skinned the lamb and cut it into pieces. Then the priests arranged the pieces on the burning fire of the altar while Father washed the inner parts and the legs. Finally, those were burned, too. As Father turned and walked back to his family, they saw blood on his robe. They understood the seriousness of the sin problem as they observed this messy, violent death. The walk home was solemn as they thought about the sacrifice. Tali had only one question.

"Why did you put your hand on the lamb's head, Abba?"

"By putting my hand on the head of the lamb, I was identifying our family with the lamb. God then accepted the lamb on our behalf so that when it died, it died as a substitute for us, making us right with God."

"I'm glad God made a way for us to be forgiven. And I'm glad you obeyed Him, Abba."

---

5 This fictional story which communicates the facts of Leviticus 1 and the significance of the sacrifices made at the Tabernacle is based on what a real person who lived during the Exodus (Numbers 1) might have experienced.

God established a process that made it possible for Israelites to have their sins forgiven near the entrance of the Tabernacle.

The Day of Atonement

Yom Kippur had arrived. Ahira[6] watched nervously as he waited to do the task for which he had been chosen.

Yom Kippur—Day of Atonement. Such a unique concept. Ahira knew that this first Day of Atonement was to be followed by many, many more. Once a year they were not to work and were to go without eating to show their sorrow for their sins.

He watched as Aaron presented two goats to the LORD at the entrance to the Tent of Meeting, and one was chosen to die. Aaron turned and motioned to Ahira, who quickly approached Aaron and took the rope of the other goat. He then stepped back, pulling the goat with him, and continued to watch.

Aaron slit the throat of the first goat, and his son caught the blood in the bowl. Then Aaron took the bowl into the Tent of Meeting. Ahira could no longer see Aaron, but he knew what was happening inside the tent.

Aaron would open the veil and enter the Most Holy Place— something that would only happen on this day each year. Once inside, Aaron would sprinkle blood on the Mercy Seat and in front of it. He had to do this to purify the Most Holy Place which was contaminated by the uncleanness and rebellion of the Israelites.

Aaron stepped back out of the tent. Ahira breathed in sharply and realized that he had been holding his breath. He watched as Aaron now sprinkled blood around the Tent of Meeting. This, too, needed to be purified because it sat every day in the midst of their uncleanness. Finally, Aaron approached the altar and purified it, too, with the blood. In fact, the Law requires that nearly everything be cleansed with blood and without the shedding of blood there is no forgiveness.[7]

Now Aaron approached Ahira. He realized it was time for his part. He stood firm with the second goat.

Ahira watched as Aaron laid both hands on the head of the goat. His mouth was moving, but the words—the groaning—were barely audible. Ahira knew that Aaron was confessing over this goat the wickedness and rebellion of the Israelites. He confessed all their sins and put them on the goat's head. Not all could see, but Ahira noticed the tears streaming down Aaron's cheeks. Ahira, moved by the scene and sensing its importance not only for Israel but also for himself, felt his own tears coursing down his cheeks. Then Aaron rose, looked at Ahira, and nodded.

Ahira led the goat out of the courtyard. Everyone watched solemnly as he walked the goat to the edge of the camp. Ahira continued walking out into the wilderness. How far should he go? Ahira wasn't sure, but he knew he was to take the goat into the wilderness and release it. He walked for several hours. Finally he stopped, knelt down, and untied the rope from the goat's neck. He ran his fingers along its back, then gave it a pat, and commanded, "Go on! Go!"

He watched as the goat bounded up a hill and down the other side, out of sight, carrying on itself all their sins. Ahira stood there, looking out over the wilderness where the goat had gone. After a while he lifted his eyes toward Heaven and breathed a prayer of thanks to God for providing a way for him—for all of Israel—to be made right with Himself. Then Ahira turned around and headed back to camp.

---

6 A fictional story portraying the truths of Leviticus 16.
7 Hebrews 9:22.

The LORD appointed an annual holy day when the contamination caused by the sins of the people would be cleansed from the Tabernacle and the sins of God's people would be removed from them.

Unbelief at Kadesh

About a year after Israel first camped in front of Mt. Sinai, the cloud above the Meeting Tent lifted, so the Israelites broke camp and left the Sinai Desert. They followed the cloud northward until it reached the Paran Desert.

Then, at Kadesh-Barnea, the LORD said to Moses, "Choose a leader from each tribe and send them into Canaan to explore the land I am giving you Israelites." (This is the land God promised to Abraham's descendants over 600 years before.) So the chosen men explored the land from the Zin Desert in the south to Rehob in the north. They found the land fruitful and the cities fortified. The men brought back some of the fruit—such as they had never seen before!

The leaders came back to Kadesh in the Paran Desert where the people were camped and gave a report. "Look at this fruit! The land we explored truly is rich with milk and honey. But the people are strong, living in large, walled cities. Several different nations are living throughout the land."

Caleb calmed down the crowd and shouted, "Let's go take possession of the land now. I know we can do it!"

But the other leaders who went with him, said, "We'll never be able to take that land. The people are too strong for us. And they're huge! We felt like grasshoppers next to them."

So the people cried all night and complained to Moses and Aaron, "We wish we had died in Egypt or somewhere out in this desert! Is the LORD leading us into Canaan to have us killed by warriors, our wives and children taken captive? We'd be better off in Egypt." Then they said to each other, "Hey, why don't we choose a leader and go back there?"

Couldn't they just believe God's Word? Couldn't they trust in Him who had promised them the land and brought them safely this far?

Well, they didn't want to go into the land, and they got their wish. God told Moses to convey this message to the people: "Not one of you will enter the land that I solemnly swore to give you except for Caleb and Joshua. You will all die here in the desert. Your children will suffer for your unfaithfulness, too. They will wander as shepherds in the desert 40 long years until the last of your generation falls dead."

Unbelief brought dreadful consequences.

From Mt. Sinai the LORD led the Israelites to the border of the land He had promised them, but they chose to not believe that He could give them the land.

The Bronze Serpent

The LORD cared for His people while they wandered for 38 years, always providing food and water for them. They never lacked anything. Yet they complained several times.

Then finally the LORD sent them toward the northern end of the Gulf of Aqaba (the southern end of Edom) to circumvent Edom, go around to the east side of the mountains, and prepare to enter the Promised Land.

But as they traveled, the people became impatient and complained against God and Moses again. "Did you bring us up from Egypt just to let us die out here in the desert? There's no water! And we loathe this miserable food!"

The LORD had had enough. He sent poisonous snakes that bit the people, and many died.

Then some of the people admitted to Moses, "We were wrong to speak against the LORD and against you. Pray to Him that He will take these snakes away."

So Moses prayed for the people, and the LORD answered:

"Make a bronze snake and put it on a pole. Anyone who is bitten can look at the snake and not die."

Moses obeyed God, crafting a snake and mounting it high on a pole. Then everyone who was bitten by a snake and looked at the bronze snake lived. It was so simple. But faith is simple. They simply had to believe what God said ("Look at the bronze snake, and live.") was true.

After this, the LORD told Moses to head to the Abarim Mountains. There He would show Moses before he died the land He would give to the Israelites.

Moses was concerned for the people. He prayed, "O God, You know the hearts of all men. Appoint a leader for the people when I die so they won't be like sheep without a shepherd."

The LORD responded, "Joshua, the son of Nun, has the right kind of heart; he can do the job. Lay your hands on him and commission him before the people as their new leader. Let the Israelites know that they must obey him now."

On their way toward Canaan, the Israelites rebelled against God and were punished with deadly serpent bites, but God graciously provided a remedy for their afflictions.

Preparation for Canaan

Near the end of the fortieth year since the Israelites left Egypt, they stood poised on the east bank of the Jordan, ready to enter the land. But the LORD God knew that the nations they were about to dispossess worshiped many false gods. So God told Moses to teach the Law to this new generation of Israelites. The lengthy message Moses expounded east of the Jordan in the territory of Moab can be found in the book of Deuteronomy (Second Law) along with a brief recap of the wilderness history. Here are high points of his message.

"The LORD your God says you must teach your children and your grandchildren in your new land across the Jordan so that you and they will fear the LORD your God all your lives and keep His commands. Then you will enjoy a long life."

"Hear, O Israel: The LORD our God, the LORD is one. Love Him with all your heart, soul, and strength. When He brings you into the land He promised to Abraham, Isaac, and Jacob and now gives to you, never forget Him. It is He who brought you out of your slavery in Egypt."

"When you received the Law on Mt. Horeb and the LORD spoke out of the fire, you didn't see any form. So be careful: don't corrupt yourselves by making idols of any shape—man, woman, animal, bird, or fish. And when you look up at the sun, moon, and stars, don't be tempted to bow down to them."

"Destroy, break down, smash, burn, and cut down all the worship places and idols of the false gods of the nations you are dispossessing. Wipe out their names from those places. Do not worship the LORD your God the way those nations worship their gods. God will establish a place for worship."

"If a prophet or dream-teller announces miraculous signs and wonders and says, 'Let us worship other gods,' do not listen to him even if the sign comes to pass. Don't learn the detestable ways of the nations in your new land. Don't sacrifice your sons and daughters in the fire, or practice sorcery, or cast spells, or call on spirits, or engage in witchcraft. The LORD is disgusted with anyone who does these things. That's why He is helping you destroy the nations in the land. They do all these things, but God does not permit you to do them. The LORD your God will raise up a prophet like me from among your people. Do what He says."

Then Moses climbed to the top of Mt. Pisgah, and the LORD showed him the whole land He had promised to Abraham, Isaac, and Jacob; and there Moses died.

Before Moses died, he had placed his hands on Joshua, and the LORD had given Joshua wisdom. The people listened to Joshua and obeyed the commands the LORD had given Moses.

The LORD God's final assignment for Moses was to teach God's Law to this new generation of Israelites, in order to prepare them to enter the pagan land of Canaan.

Conquest of the Promised Land

After Moses died, the LORD spoke to Joshua, "Moses my servant is dead. Now get ready to take all these people across the Jordan River into the land I promised to give them. No one will be able to defeat you. As I was with Moses, so I will be with you. Be strong and courageous because it is you who will lead these people into the land I swore to give to their ancestors."

And God worked just as He declared He would. First, a prostitute named Rahab from Jericho changed her mind about following other gods before the Israelites even took the land saying, "I know the LORD has given this land to you … the LORD your God is God of all." Then, God made it so the Israelites could cross the Jordan on dry ground. He made the walls of Jericho fall miraculously, and He defeated Jericho and all Israel's enemies so that Joshua took the entire land. Then he divided the territory among Israel's tribes, and they had peace in the land.

Near the end of Joshua's life, the LORD told the Israelites a story through their leader. Joshua called the people together at Shechem and told them, "This is what the LORD, the God of Israel says:

'Long ago your ancestors, including Abraham, his father and brother, lived on the other side of the Euphrates and worshiped other gods. I took Abraham away from there and brought him to Canaan. I gave him Isaac as the first of a long line of descendants. To Isaac I gave Jacob and Esau. I had Esau settle in the hill country of Seir, but Jacob took his family down to Egypt.

'Later I sent Moses to help your people. I made all those horrible things happen to the Egyptians and brought your ancestors out of Egypt. The Egyptians came after your ancestors, trapping them at the Red Sea. Your people cried to Me for help, so I came between them and the Egyptians in a cloud and opened the sea so they could walk through on dry ground. The Egyptians tried to follow, but I brought the water back and buried them. You lived in the desert for a long time.

'Then I brought you to the land east of the Jordan and helped you defeat the people there. After that, you crossed the Jordan. I gave all those peoples over to you, and you defeated them.

'Now you live in towns you didn't build and eat grapes and olives from vineyards and trees you didn't plant. You didn't have to work for this land; I gave it to you.'"

After Joshua walked them through God's brief synopsis, he lifted his voice and challenged them.

"Worship the LORD and fear Him. Get rid of the idols your ancestors worshiped when they lived on the other side of the Euphrates and in Egypt, and serve the LORD alone. But if you don't want to worship the LORD God, decide now! Do you want to worship the gods of your ancestors or the gods of the people you dispossessed from this land? Not me! My family and I will worship and obey the LORD."

The people responded saying, "We could never worship other gods. The LORD is our God."

Not long afterward, God's servant Joshua died at the age of 110.

After the death of Moses, Joshua led the Israelites across the Jordan River and into the promised land of Canaan, which they conquered with the help of the LORD their God.

The Judges, an Era of Spiritual Darkness

***The Prayer of an Israelite Living More Than
300 Years after Joshua's Death[8]***

O LORD God, help us! I don't pray for deliverance from the Philistines but from our apostasy. We have forsaken You and turned to false gods—and so many times! Up, down, up, down, like a bucket in a well has been our history. We turned from You and followed other gods; You sent oppressors. We cried out to You, and You so faithfully sent deliverers—six of them now (Othniel, Ehud, Deborah and Barak, Gideon, Jephthah, and Samson)—You are so faithful! But after You delivered us through Your leader, it wasn't long before we turned away from You to other gods again. Will we never learn?

We have not listened. We have turned away from You. We all do what we think is right.

You sent Your angel to us just after we had conquered the land. You reminded us of Your faithfulness in bringing us to the land, fulfilling Your covenant. But we disobeyed: we did not break down the foreign altars as You required. I remember Your words delivered on that occasion; my great-grandfather always recounted them with tears as he quoted his father's telling of the event: "Why have you done this?" I don't know why, LORD. How could we have been so quick to forget what You asked of us and what we said we would do?

Now these people have been thorns in our side and their "gods" a snare to us, testing us time and time again to see if we will be faithful. We have not been faithful, LORD. We have forsaken You and served the Baals and the Ashtoreths. These Phoenician gods are not the "storm god," nor the "queen of heaven"; they are simply pieces of wood carved by humans to look like humans. They are not fertility gods. Only You, LORD, can give and take life.

Deliver us, O LORD, again I say, not from our oppressors but from our apostasy. Deliver us from this downward-spiraling, sin-driven cycle. May we worship You alone. You are the LORD, our God.

---

8 An imagined prayer based on and conveying the facts found in the book of Judges.

After Joshua died, the Israelites were ruled by various tribal rulers known as "judges" and the lack of good central leadership contributed to moral and political chaos.

Some Bright Lights in an Era of Darkness

Entries in Ruth's Diary[9]

… Today I nearly vomited during worship time. I always knew that our national god, Chemosh, accepted human sacrifices, but I had never seen it. I was horrified as they laid that screaming baby on the burning coals. And the only other person weeping was the infant's mother! …

… As we returned from worship today, the streets were full of people from different lands. We had heard of the famine in neighboring countries, but are just now seeing its results …

… Today I watched through the curtain as Father talked with Naomi about me becoming her son Mahlon's wife. His father died a short time ago. He seems nice. I could do worse. I hope I can be a comfort to him during this difficult time in his life. Being married to a foreigner may have its difficulties …

… Life goes on. I love being married to Mahlon. He treats me well, as does Naomi, but they will not come to worship Chemosh. It's just as well—more human sacrifices today. Mahlon and his mother talk of a different god. They say their god is the one, true, living god. At least that is something—to not have to pray to a carved stick or a piece of rock. I want to know more …

… We celebrated our tenth anniversary today! Still no child. But I myself feel like a brand-new baby—I finally said "no" to Chemosh and "yes" to the LORD God of the Israelites. I now belong to Him.

… Mahlon died during the night. My heart aches. It's hard to believe that he is … gone. I turn to his God and this is the way He treats me? No, I need to trust Him. I don't understand what He is doing but …

… Today Naomi told me she is going back to Israel. They have food there now. I don't know if I can lose her, too, I love her so …

.. I started on a new adventure today. As my sister-in-law and I accompanied Naomi, she tried to send me back three times—insisting on my best interests. But I told her, "Your people will be my people and your God my God." We arrived in Bethlehem today at the beginning of barley harvest…

… I haven't written for a while. I've been working hard and God is blessing. I began gleaning in Boaz' field and we have had more than enough to eat. He is so kind …

… Naomi wants me to get dressed up and lie at Boaz' feet tonight. As a near relative he could be the one to marry me and give me children for Mahlon's line. He'll either reject me or accept me …

… He didn't throw me out! We are to be married soon …

… It's been more than nine months since I've written and guess what? I have a son. We named him Obed …

… Many years have passed. I found you today, diary, and read through you. I do not have much more time on this earth now. Obed, our son has his own son, Jesse. But it is not about him that I write today. I write about my great-grandson. Yes, Jesse and his wife have one more son (They already had seven!). This one is special. I believe he will do great things. His name is David.

---

9 Ruth was a Moabitess who lived during the time of Israel's judges. She is one of few shining stars during that dark period of history. These fictitious entries that she could have written in her diary tell the story found in the book of Ruth.

Samuel, the final judge of Israel, was faithful to the LORD God, as were Boaz and Ruth, the Moabite woman whom Boaz married.

Saul, Israel's First King

Samuel grew up serving the LORD and became Israel's best leader, presiding over disputes among the people for many years. Samuel communicated God's revelation to the people. Although not a military leader, Samuel was instrumental in the Israelites' deliverance from the Philistines.

One day the leaders came to him and said, "Samuel, we want a king to lead us like the other nations have." Samuel was crushed! He went to the LORD for guidance.

"Samuel," God replied, "give them what they ask. They are not rejecting you, but Me as their king. Ever since I rescued them from Egypt, they have turned from Me to idols. Go ahead, give them a king, but warn them first about how a king will treat them."

God sent Saul, a good-looking Benjamite who stood head and shoulders above the others, to Samuel to be appointed as king. Samuel anointed him with oil and said, "You are the one God has chosen to lead and rule His people." That very day the Spirit of God came on him powerfully, transforming his heart.

Saul started out well, humbly serving God as king of His people for more than two years. But he was impatient and acted foolishly, assuming the role of a priest. So God, through Samuel, told him he would not continue as king, nor would his descendants sit on the throne. Then one day he outright disobeyed God, sparing the best of the spoils from a battle with one of Israel's enemies. Making matters worse, he lied about it, saying he had spared the animals to sacrifice them to the LORD.

Samuel brought God's response: "Does the LORD really want sacrifices and burnt offerings? No. He would rather you obey Him. Disobedience and rebellion are as bad in God's eyes as worshiping idols or practicing witchcraft. Since you rejected God's Word, He has rejected you as king."

Distraught, Saul admitted, "I was wrong. Please forgive me so things can be different."

"You disobeyed; it's decided."

As Samuel turned to leave, Saul caught the edge of Samuel's robe, and it tore! Samuel turned and declared, "The LORD has torn the kingdom of Israel from you today and will give it to someone better."

The LORD sent Samuel to Bethlehem, the house of Ruth's grandson, Jesse, to anoint a new king. He met the firstborn—good-looking and tall like Saul. Samuel thought, "This must be the one!"

But God said, "Don't think he is the one just because he's tall and handsome. I have not chosen him. People judge others by what they look like, but I judge them by what is in their hearts."

Samuel met all of Jesse's sons that day, but it wasn't until they brought the youngest from tending the sheep (His father hadn't even brought him inside!) that he met Israel's future king. David was brought in and God told Samuel, "Get up and anoint him. He's the one."

Samuel anointed David in front of all his brothers. The Spirit of the LORD came upon David from that day forward. David served King Saul in the palace and served in the army and was so successful people sang his praises! Angered and suspicious, Saul kept a jealous eye on David from then on.

In spite of the fact that God was their King and Samuel was one of Israel's best leaders, the Israelites asked for a king and in response God gave them Saul.

OLD
TESTAMENT

CREATION

FALL

FLOOD

BABEL

PATRIARCHS

MOSES

JOSHUA

JUDGES

MONARCHY

DIVISION

EXILE

RETURN

King David, a Special King for Israel

Did you ever think, "What is God doing? Has He forgotten His promises?" Sometimes it's tempting to think that way, but God is faithful and carries out His plans.

Jacob predicted that the scepter would not depart from Judah—more than 800 years before Israel ever had a king, his lineage was predicted. About 750 years later, Samuel's mother, in a prayer of grateful praise, declared, "O LORD, You will give power to Your king and strength to the one You anoint." Just a few decades later, Samuel was anointing an obscure shepherd from the tribe of Judah to be king over Israel. And oh, the covenant God would make with David not many years hence!

David had served the LORD and experienced His power as a young shepherd on the hills of Bethlehem, killing wild animals that attacked his sheep! But it wasn't until he killed a Philistine giant who was intimidating Israel's army that he burst on the public scene. From that time on, people couldn't get enough of him, except for Saul. Even though David faithfully served him as God's chosen king, Saul was jealous of David's popularity and tried to kill him several times. But David remained loyal, passing up at least two opportunities to kill Saul.

Several years after Saul died in battle and just after his sole surviving son was assassinated by rogues, all the tribes of Israel anointed David as king (again). When he marched on Jerusalem and captured the city, it became known as "The City of David." Then he brought the ark of God to the city, built a palace, and enjoyed God-given peace.

At that time David said to Nathan the prophet, "Something's wrong! I live in a beautiful house and the ark of God sits in a tent." The LORD gave a message to Nathan.

"Go tell my servant David this is God's answer: 'Do I need you to build a house for Me? I don't need a house and I never asked anyone to build Me one. This tent has been fine for Me to dwell with My people.

'Here is what I, the LORD All-Powerful, want you to know: I took you, a nobody following sheep around the countryside, and made you king over My people, defeated your enemies, and will make you one of the most famous people in the world. I've given My people a place to live and peace with their enemies.

'I will establish a house[10] for you. I promise that you and your descendants will be kings. I will choose one of your sons to be king when you die and make him a great ruler. No one will be able to take his kingdom away from him. He will build Me a temple.

'When he does wrong, I will correct him as parents correct their children, but I will never put an end to this covenant, nor will I take the kingdom away from you like I did with Saul. I guarantee that one of your descendants will always be king.'"

---

10 God uses "house" here in the sense of dynasty.

After several years of protecting himself from Saul, David emerged as a great king of Israel and the LORD promised to establish the throne of his kingdom forever.

David's Messianic Psalms

David, the mighty warrior, became a great king. He also was a musician and wrote many songs called psalms under the influence of the Holy Spirit of God. Sometimes David used his songs to praise God for His goodness and protection. Other times he cried out for forgiveness of his sins. Still other times he complained to God about the situation in which he found himself. David wrote his songs about his own personal struggles and victories; he had plenty! But the lyrics of some of his songs deal with grander (and more horrific!) situations than David ever experienced. In these instances David was writing about a person who was to live on this earth after him—about a promised one who would come later. David was prophesying about a future deliverer. Because of God's covenant with David, David knew that God would deliver his descendant(s) from trouble and suffering just as he had delivered David.

Speaking or writing about someone who would come to deliver God's people was not new. God first spoke of a person when He told Adam and his wife that from Eve would come one who would defeat Satan. God also spoke of blessing all families of the earth through a future descendant of Abraham. Someone special was referred to when Jacob declared that the scepter would never depart from Judah and later when Nathan told of the unending reign of David's line. Even Moses' proclamation of a future prophet who would instruct the people foresaw the coming of a significantly different, important person.

All this foretelling of someone special who would deliver or bless or reign brought hope to God's people. As time passed, those Israelites who were serious about all that the Lord had said and who thought deeply about it began to realize that the LORD's plan to provide lasting hope and joy for mankind was focusing on one special person whom they referred to as the Messiah ("anointed one").

Through David's songs about that person, the general identity and intended roles of God's Messiah became increasingly clear. These songs came to be known as Messianic Psalms. Among other things, these songs tell us that the Messiah will be a powerful ruler whom the enemies of the LORD will fear. And yet, they also tell of one who will be humiliated, suffer greatly—even die—at the hands of his enemies.[11] How can this be? Who can this be?

---

11 For two examples of Messianic Psalms, read Psalm 2 and Psalm 22.

David, the great soldier and king, was also a musician who wrote many psalms (songs), several of which prophesied that the LORD would send a Messiah who would suffer and reign.

King Solomon, David's Son

David's son, Solomon, succeeded his father as king of Israel. When Solomon took the throne, the LORD appeared to him! "What shall I give you? Ask."

Solomon showed great character in his reply. Gratefully, he began, "You were so kind to my father, David, throughout his life, and now You've given him an heir for his throne." He humbly continued, "I am young and unsure in my new responsibilities." He wisely and unselfishly requested, "Please give me a discerning heart to lead Your people well, distinguishing between right and wrong."

God was pleased with Solomon's request and granted it. The LORD made Solomon wiser than anyone in the world!

Now Israel was located in the middle of the trade routes. Anyone going from the west (Egypt, Africa, etc.) went right through Israel or Edom (which Solomon also controlled at this time) to get to the east (Assyria, Babylon, etc.), and vice versa. So people began to hear about Solomon's wisdom, and they came to hear him. This accomplished God's plan. He had said to Moses that He wanted Israel to be a kingdom of priests and a holy nation.

Solomon wrote 3,000 proverbs and 1,005 songs. Many of these are in the Bible, God's Word. His book called "Proverbs" contains wisdom for the nations. His book, Ecclesiastes, can be summed up by this statement: "You can have it all, but without God you have nothing." The Song of Solomon tells readers that marriage and its bed can be wonderful.

Solomon also built the Temple for God that his father, David, wanted to build. In his prayer of dedication he declared, "O LORD God of Israel, there is none like You in Heaven or on earth. The highest heaven cannot contain You—how could this Temple I have built? But hear the prayers of Your people when they pray toward this place. And when we sin, but have a change of heart and turn back to You, forgive our wickedness. Be open to my plea and to the plea of Your people because You have chosen us from all the nations of the world. Turn our hearts to You, LORD, to walk in Your ways and keep Your commands so that all the peoples of the earth may know that You are God and that there is no other."

What a prayer! What a start Solomon had! But Solomon loved many foreign women from the nations from which God had commanded the Israelites not to marry because they would turn their hearts after false gods. And that is exactly what happened. His wives (He had hundreds!) turned his heart after other gods so that he was not fully devoted to the LORD his God. The king of the nation that was to show the peoples of the earth that "the LORD is God and there is no other," followed Ashtoreth, goddess of the Sidonians, and Molech, the detestable god of the Ammonites.

Solomon displeased God with his foolish ways. He did not follow God completely, as David his father had done.

Solomon succeeded his father, David, as king and ruled over Israel at the height of its wealth and power, during which time he built the Temple for the LORD that David had wanted.

The Kingdom of Israel Divided

Solomon's unfaithfulness to God affected the people of Israel. They worshiped Ashtoreth (goddess of the Sidonians), Chemosh (god of the Moabites), and Molech (god of the Ammonites). Turning from God to false gods is called apostasy. God's people turned away time and time again. Something had to be done.

The LORD was angry with Solomon. God had appeared twice to him and still he turned his heart away and followed other gods. God told him, "I will surely tear the kingdom away from you and give it to your servant. Yet, for your father's sake, I will not do this during your lifetime. Your son will pay because I will rip the kingdom from his hand. Still, I will only take part of the kingdom from him. In honor of my servant David and respect for my chosen city Jerusalem I will leave one tribe."[12]

One day, Jeroboam, an official in Solomon's administration, was leaving Jerusalem. A prophet named Ahijah, wearing a brand-new coat, met him on the road. He took off his coat and ripped it into twelve pieces. Then he said to Jeroboam, "Take 10 pieces for yourself. God says, 'Look, I'm going to tear the kingdom out of Solomon's hand and give you 10 tribes because they have forsaken me and worshiped other gods. They don't follow Me or obey my laws as David did.'"

Rehoboam, Solomon's son, succeeded him as king, but shortly after that, the kingdom was divided—10 tribes followed Jeroboam, 2 stayed with Rehoboam. The 10 tribes in the north kept the name Israel while the 2 in the south became known as Judah.

Since the Temple was in Jerusalem, Jeroboam was afraid that his people would go there to worship and eventually give their allegiance to Rehoboam since he was king of the nation that housed the LORD's Temple. So soon after Jeroboam became king of Israel, he made two golden calves and told the people, "It's too hard to go to Jerusalem to worship. Israel, here are your gods who brought you out of Egypt." He set one up in Bethel in the south and the other in the northern city of Dan. The people sinned by worshiping these idols.

Sadly, both of the nations continued to follow idols and false gods, breaking God's first two commands. Because of this, Ahijah predicted to Jeroboam's wife that Israel would be uprooted from their promised land and scattered.

Yes, judgment was coming. In about 200 years the northern kingdom would no longer exist. Every one of its 20 kings was evil and did not serve the LORD God.

The southern kingdom continued for nearly 350 years with more than half of its kings being wicked. However, some of Judah's kings served the LORD.

---

12 Judah is the one tribe that remained along with Benjamin, which had been absorbed into Judah.

Because Solomon worshiped false gods late in his life, God took 10 of the tribes of Israel from Solomon's son Rehoboam and gave them to a man named Jeroboam.

OLD
TESTAMENT

CREATION
FALL
FLOOD
BABEL
PATRIARCHS
MOSES
JOSHUA
JUDGES
MONARCHY
DIVISION
EXILE
RETURN

God's Prophets Elijah & Elisha

Noah, Moses, Samuel, and Ahijah were prophets (messengers) from God. During the time of the divided kingdom pagan religions influenced Israel and Judah. But God did not abandon them. He sent prophets to speak for Him, of whom Elijah (Yahweh is God) was one.

Ahab became king over Israel, reigning in Samaria. He was the worst king yet. Ahab married Jezebel, the daughter of the king of Sidon, and began to serve and worship Baal, the supreme god of the Canaanites, who was supposedly the god of rain and weather.

Elijah declared to Ahab, "Just as the LORD, the God of Israel lives, whom I serve, a drought is coming for several years. You won't see a drop of rain or dew unless I say otherwise." The people had a choice: follow the "god of rain and weather" or the LORD, the one true and living God.

After three and a half years of no rain, Ahab met Elijah again. "Is that you, troublemaker?"

Elijah replied, "I haven't troubled Israel. You and your family have, abandoning the LORD and following the Baals. Now call the people together from all over Israel to Mount Carmel, and be sure to bring the 450 prophets of Baal."

When they met on the mountain, Elijah challenged the people, "How long will you waver? If the LORD is the true God, follow Him. But if it's Baal, follow him. Decide!" The people kept quiet.

Elijah continued. "I'm the only one of the LORD's prophets left. Baal has 450. Get us two bulls. They can choose the one they want, cut it in pieces, and put it on the wood, but not set fire to it. I'll do the same with the other bull. Then call to Baal, and I'll call on the name of the LORD. The god who answers by fire—he is God." The people agreed.

The prophets of Baal prepared their bull and called to Baal all morning long. "O Baal, answer us!" No response. They danced. No response.

Elijah taunted them. "Shout louder! Maybe your god is deep in thought, or traveling, or sleeping." They shouted louder and cut themselves. Their blood flowed. Midday passed. Still no response.

Elijah addressed all the people. "Enough. Come here." The people came and watched as he repaired the altar of the LORD which was in ruins. He dug a trench around the altar. He arranged the wood, killed and cut up the bull, and laid it on the wood. Then he said, "Fill four large jars with water and pour it on the offering and on the wood." They did. "Do it again." They did it again. "Do it once more." They poured the water a third time so that it ran down the altar and filled the trench.

Then Elijah prayed: "O God, God of Abraham, Isaac, and Israel, let these people know now that You are God in Israel and that I am your servant. Answer. Show that You are God, the true God, and that You want them to turn back to You."

Fire flashed down from heaven, consuming the bull, the wood, the altar, the dirt, and all the water in the trench! The people saw and fell on their faces in worship. They shouted, "The LORD is God! The LORD is the true God!"

Elijah served the LORD as His prophet until God took him to Heaven in a whirlwind. Elisha, his assistant, carried on the prophetic ministry in Israel and beyond for many more years.

In an era of extreme spiritual darkness in the northern kingdom of Israel, the LORD God raised up Elijah and Elisha, two prophets who denounced the idolatrous false religion of their times.

Pre-Exilic Prophecies of Israel & Judah

Even though God sent His prophets (Elijah, Elisha, and others) to proclaim His word orally, the Israelites continued to turn away from God. So God sent prophets who not only spoke His word to the people, but also wrote it down for them. These prophets[13] pronounced future judgment for the sins of Israel, Judah, and other nations, but they also wrote of one who would come to solve the sin problem once and for all—the Messiah (God's anointed one).

Many facts about Messiah were revealed in the writings of these prophets, but always within the historical context of the day. For example …

… God told Ahaz, king of Judah, to ask for a sign of deliverance from Assyria. In false piety, Ahaz refused. God determined to give him one. The prophecy given that day provided Ahaz with a sign, but also revealed that the Messiah would come from David's line and have a unique birth (see Isaiah 7:13-14).

… Assyria had laid siege to Jerusalem. Food was scarce. Would they survive? A prophecy was given revealing that the Messiah would come from Bethlehem (House of Bread and David's ancestral home). Even though Israel would fall soon and suffer for a time, this one would eventually rule Israel and if anyone like the Assyrians came along during His reign, He would send them packing (see Micah 5:1-6).

… The Assyrians, coming from the north, were threatening Israel and Judah, but the region of Galilee was especially distressed, walking in the gloom and darkness of their oppressors. Isaiah prophesied that the son of David would come and shine a great light on those living in the shadow of death (see Isaiah 9:1-5).

… In the midst of war and oppression, it appeared as if the kingdom would be lost forever. The prophecy was given that the Messiah's kingdom would never end; he would reign in peace and glory from David's throne forever (see Isaiah 9:6).

But the most confusing—and exciting—of all were the prophecies that spoke of the sufferings of the Messiah and the blessings resulting from those sufferings:

- He would be disfigured and marred beyond human likeness … to cleanse the nations
- He would be pierced … to pay for our rebellion
- He would be crushed … to pay for our sins
- He would be punished … to bring us peace
- He would be wounded … to heal us
- He would suffer, be crushed, killed … and live again
- His soul would suffer and die, then see the light of life (!) … to justify many and bear their sins (see Isaiah 52-53).

As Israel and Judah continued to deteriorate, the LORD raised up other prophets who foretold in writing the demise of those kingdoms, as well as the coming of the Messiah.

---

13 The writings of 16 of these prophets are preserved for us in the latter part of the Old Testament.

The Exiles of Israel & Judah

Even though the LORD God had delivered them from the power of Pharaoh in Egypt and proved His power and love to His people time and again, the northern kingdom of Israel sinned against Him. They worshiped other gods and followed the customs of the ungodly nations whom the LORD had driven out of the land. Israel's kings even encouraged this pagan worship and introduced additional practices.

The LORD was very angry with the people of Israel and rejected them, removing them from His presence by giving them into the hands of plunderers. The king of Assyria invaded the land, marching against the capital, Samaria, and laid siege to it for three years. Finally, in the year 722 B.C., he captured the city and deported the Israelites to Assyria. Then the king of Assyria brought people from cities throughout the Assyrian Empire and settled them in the towns of Samaria. These foreigners replaced the Israelites and took over the whole area. One of the exiled priests returned to Bethel to teach these people how to worship the LORD, but each nationality still made their own gods and continued to worship them.

This left only Judah, the southern kingdom, but they did not obey the LORD's commands either. They walked in the customs which Israel introduced. So 134 years later, God's judgment fell on them as well. Nebuchadnezzar and his entire Babylonian army (Babylon had subsequently conquered Assyria) marched on and laid siege to Jerusalem, the capital of Judah. For nearly two years the people of Jerusalem were trapped, and eventually they had nothing to eat. Finally the wall was broken through, but Zedekiah (the king of Judah) fled with all his warriors. The Babylonians pursued Zedekiah, scattered his army, captured him, and killed his sons right before his eyes. The brutal murder of his sons was the last thing Zedekiah saw. They immediately blinded him and led him bound to Babylon.

Later, Nebuchadnezzar's chief deputy arrived in Jerusalem. He burned the Temple, the royal palace, and the whole city to the ground. He had his soldiers break up and knock down the city walls. Then he rounded up everyone who was left in the city and led them off into exile. The only ones left were a few poor farmers to tend what remained in the fields and vineyards.

In the meantime, the Babylonians broke up the bronze pillars, washstands, and the huge basin that were in the Temple of the LORD and took it to Babylon. They plundered so much bronze that they couldn't even weigh it! They also gathered all the bronze, silver, and gold liturgical accessories that had been used in worship at the Temple and hauled it off to Babylon.

So Judah was exiled from the land and the Temple was destroyed and plundered.

But how can this be? God had promised David that He would establish his house (dynasty) forever. God had said that when David's offspring disobeyed, they would be punished, but that His love would not be removed from him as occurred with Saul. One of David's offspring would succeed him and have a kingdom and throne which God would establish forever. Had God broken His promise? Did He not really promise David's house would endure forever? And what of the Temple? Solomon had mentioned in his prayer of dedication that the Temple was to be a testimony to the LORD's uniqueness as the only God. What did its destruction portend?

Or is it possible that the overthrow of the Davidic line of kings would be temporary? Is it possible that the son whose throne would be established forever had not yet come on the scene?

The kingdoms of Israel and Judah both continued to deteriorate spiritually and the LORD God punished them with exile in Assyria and Babylonia.

Exilic Prophecies from Judah

***An Interview with the Prophet Jeremiah near
the End of His Life in Tahpanhes, Egypt[14]***

When were you called into the prophetic ministry?
The word of the LORD first came to me when I was about 20 years
old. Good king Josiah had been reigning for 13 years. After that I
prophesied during the reigns of the final five kings of Judah before the
exile.

**People have called you the "Weeping Prophet" and the
"Lonely Prophet." Why is that?** Some called me the lonely prophet
because God told me not to marry. Actually I was not to get married,
take part in any festive occasions, or even participate in funerals—to
be a vivid warning to Judah that captivity was coming. The weeping
prophet? That relates to the awful message I brought to Judah of the
coming destruction. Several times I said something like "If you won't
listen, my soul will sob in secret for such pride and my eyes will bitterly
weep and flow down with tears …" My eyes were like fountains. Oh,
that Judah would have listened!

Were you ever scared? I knew that a terrible destruction
was coming to Judah—I was imprisoned, then kidnapped and taken
to Egypt. Wouldn't you be frightened? But I kept trusting in what
God told me so many years ago when He called me. I told Him I was
too young and couldn't do it. He said, "Don't say you're just a boy. I
will tell you where to go and what to say—and you will go there and
say it! Don't be afraid of anyone. I will take care of you."

**Wow! You can't go wrong with that. That brings me to
my last question: which do you think were your most significant
prophecies?** There were some important ones, like the curse on
Jeconiah. And there were warnings—so many warnings against
sin and judgment. But God also gave me a message of hope and
restoration to communicate. In all that, I would have to say there are
three that stand out for me.

First is the duration of the captivity. Yes, the Babylonians
captured us, destroying the Temple and the city, but God said that
after 70 years He would punish Babylon and bring His people home.
He told of plans He has for us that include a hopeful future. He made
it clear that if we truly seek Him with all our heart we will find Him.

I think the Messianic prediction God gave through me
would have to be another of the most important prophecies I
shared. God declared: "The time is coming when I will raise up a
truly righteous Branch from David's line that will reign wisely and do
what is right in the land, saving both Judah and Israel." His ministry
will be so significant that the catchphrase "As sure as the Lord lives
that brought Israel out of Egypt" will be changed to "As sure as the
Lord lives that brought back His people from all the countries where
He'd scattered them." His name will be The Lord Our Righteousness.
That is significant, praise Jehovah!

You mentioned three. What is the third? Definitely the
New Covenant God gave to His people. God started His nation with
the Abrahamic Covenant (land, descendants, blessing) and once it
was well established gave the Davidic Covenant, emphasizing the
descendant and his throne. In between these two unconditional
covenants He made the Mosaic Covenant, establishing His people
as a kingdom of priests, a holy nation who represented God to the
nations. But the Mosaic Covenant was conditional. If we obeyed
the Law, we would receive the blessings. Simple, right? But so
difficult. We couldn't keep the Law. But oh, how wonderful this New
Covenant will be! God will not write His Law on tablets of stone
again, but directly on our hearts. And that's not all. This covenant
is unconditional. Its fulfillment depends not upon us, but solely on
God's faithfulness. He said He will be our God and we His people.
He will forgive our wickedness and remember our sins no more.

The prophet Jeremiah was not taken to Babylon in the
exile but was left behind to continue his ministry, during
which time he wrote about the coming Messiah and a New
Covenant.

---

14 Although the interview is imaginary, the information communicated through it is
accurate.

Exilic Prophecies from Babylon

While Jeremiah was prophesying in the rubble of Jerusalem and Egypt, the LORD was speaking in Babylon through two of His other prophets. One of them, Ezekiel, was sharing a message with the same themes as Jeremiah. He told of a future time when God's people would no longer be pushed around. Instead, God would appoint a king from David's line to be a single shepherd over His people. And even though Ezekiel did not use the term "New Covenant," he also spoke of it, revealing the fact that during that time the LORD would give His people a new heart and put His Spirit in them to enable them to live by His commands.

Daniel (God's other prophet in Babylon) and Ezekiel were taken captive to Babylon in 605 and 597 B.C., respectively. Just as God elevated Joseph to a position of power and honor in Egypt, so He did with Daniel. God enabled him to predict the rise and fall of nations and the transfer of global power—some of which happened during his lifetime and shortly after (within 200 years), some of which is still to come.

The king of Babylon, Nebuchadnezzar, had a disturbing dream. He called on all his advisors (of which Daniel was one) to interpret the dream for him—but first they had to tell him the dream! The king offered money and rewards to the one who could tell him his dream and its interpretation. After it was clear that no one could do it, Daniel stepped forward, told the king to keep his money, and declared:

"No mere human—no wise man, enchanter, magician or diviner—can unlock this mystery. But there is a God in Heaven who unlocks mysteries. He is unlocking this one to let you know what will happen in the future. King, in your dream you saw a massive, striking, terrifying statue. Its head was made of gold, its chest and arms of silver, its belly and thighs of bronze, its legs of iron, and its feet were made of an iron/ceramic mixture. As you looked at the statue, a rock cut by invisible hands hit and smashed the feet, causing the entire statue—clay, iron, bronze, silver, and gold—to fall and break into smithereens. The wind came along and blew the statue's dust away while the rock became a huge mountain, dominating the whole earth.

"Now, king, here is what your dream means: The God of Heaven has made you a glorious, powerful king over the entire world. You are the head of gold. Another kingdom, inferior to yours, will come next. Then that kingdom will be taken over by a third—the bronze—ruling over all, followed by a fourth as strong as iron. Just as iron breaks other metals, so this kingdom will break up and smash the previous kingdoms.

"But the feet and toes (iron/ceramic mixture) will deteriorate into a hybrid kingdom which still will have some remains of iron (strong), but mixed with pottery (weak, easily broken). Eventually, the kingdom won't hold together any more than an iron/ceramic mixture can hold together.

"At that time, God will build His kingdom which will never be destroyed nor fall to another kingdom. Christ the King will crush all other kingdoms once and for all and stand for eternity just as the rock crushed the metals and filled the earth."

The king was amazed and fell on his face before Daniel, declaring, "Your God is the God of all gods and the master of all kings, revealer of mysteries."

Daniel and Ezekiel were taken as exiles to Babylon, but from there they bravely and faithfully proclaimed God's messages, including predictions of the coming Messiah.

Jews Return to Jerusalem

Remember Jeremiah's prediction that God would punish Babylon and end Judah's exile, returning them to their land after 70 years? Follow the amazing story on this story timeline.

c. 722 B.C. The king of Assyria conquers Israel and brings people from the north to live in and around Samaria. Over time they become known as Samaritans. These people are taught to worship the LORD God, but continue to make their own idols and worship them. They join their previous belief system with Judaism, forming a syncretistic counterfeit religion.[15]

c. 700 B.C. Isaiah records God's declaration that "I, your Redeemer who made you, announce, 'Jerusalem shall be inhabited, the towns of Judah built; I will restore their ruins.' Cyrus, my shepherd will do what I desire and say, 'Rebuild Jerusalem! Lay the foundations of the Temple!'" This prophecy is given even before Jerusalem is destroyed and Judah is conquered.

605 B.C. Judah is conquered by Babylon.

597, 586 B.C. Judah's nobles are taken captive to Babylon (including Daniel and Ezekiel).

580 B.C. Cyrus is born to Cambyses 1, king of Persia. Astyages, king of Media, attempts to murder Cyrus by ordering his steward to kill the baby. Unable to do so, the steward hires a shepherd to leave the baby in the desert to die. The shepherd and his wife take pity on Cyrus and rear him as their own.

539 B.C. Cyrus, now king of Persia, conquers Babylon.

539 B.C. God moves Cyrus' heart to make a proclamation: "The LORD, the God of Heaven, has given me all the kingdoms of the earth and assigned me to build His Temple in Jerusalem. If you belong to His people—God be with you—go back to Jerusalem and build!" At this point the "Israelites" become known as "Jews" because they were from Judah.

536 B.C. Zerubbabel leads 49,697 Jews from Babylon back to Judah with 5,400 gold and silver articles which had been taken from the Temple by Nebuchadnezzar. Cyrus gave them back! When they arrive in Jerusalem, the people give offerings of more than 1,000 pounds of gold and about 3 tons of silver, plus 100 priestly garments.

535 B.C. Zerubbabel and fellow priests begin the work of rebuilding the Temple (70 years after exile had begun) accompanied by vibrant worship with trumpets and cymbals, singing and shouting praise to the LORD. The Samaritans try to join in the building of the Temple. The Jews refuse, recognizing the inherent danger of worshiping with their syncretistic neighbors. The Samaritans then seek to discourage and frustrate the Jews' plans to rebuild the Temple throughout the reign of Cyrus and into the reign of King Darius of Persia.

515 B.C. The Jewish leaders finish the Temple under the leadership of the prophets Haggai and Zechariah, dedicating it in joyful celebration.

Seventy years after Daniel and other choice captives were taken to Babylon, the Persian king who had recently conquered Babylonia released the Jews to go home to rebuild their Temple.

---

15 Syncretism: combining two or more belief systems (religions).

The Walls Rebuilt & the People Revived

Nehemiah, an important Jewish official in the Persian government almost a century after nearly 50,000 Jews had returned to Jerusalem, had a visit from his brother, Hanani. Nehemiah asked his brother about the situation in Jerusalem and learned that the exile returnees in Judah were distressed, suffering appalling conditions. The walls of Jerusalem were still in ruins and the gates, ashes.

The news grieved Nehemiah greatly, so he prayed that God would give him success with a request for the king. The king asked, "Why the long face, Nehemiah?" Nehemiah told the king about the disgraceful conditions of Jerusalem. "What do you want?" the king asked. Seeing the opportunity, Nehemiah prayed a quick prayer and then asked to be sent to rebuild the walls. The king not only sent him, but gave letters of safe passage and orders for expensive materials!

When Nehemiah arrived in Jerusalem, the first thing he did was to investigate the situation. Then he called the people together and challenged them to the task. As one man, the people replied, "We're with you. Let's start rebuilding now!"

Just as with the rebuilding of the Temple, they had opposition right from the start. When the neighboring people saw the repairs going well and gaps being closed, they were angry and stirred up all the more trouble. But Nehemiah and his team prayed to the LORD, posted guards, and kept on working. They finished the wall in only 52 days! Realizing that God made it happen, the surrounding enemies cowered in fear and felt impotent before this people whose God was at work for them.

The walls were finished just before the seventh month in which God's people were to celebrate three holy days to the LORD: Trumpets, the Day of Atonement, and Tabernacles. On the first day of the month (the Feast of Trumpets) Ezra and 13 others ascended a wooden stage that had been built by the Water Gate, just south of the Temple. From there they read the Law to the people who stood and listened attentively for hours. The people responded with, "Amen! Amen!" and then bowed low to the ground and worshiped the LORD, weeping. Nehemiah, the governor, got up and told them, "Don't cry. Today is a sacred day of rejoicing!"

Three weeks later, after all the feasts, the people assembled again, this time fasting and dressed in burlap with dust on their heads as signs of repentance. They confessed their sins and the wrongdoings of their forefathers. They listened to the Word of God and then spent time in confession and worship. They had come to realize who the LORD God really is—great, mighty, awesome, holy, loving, yet a just judge, the giver of life, covenant maker and keeper, and so much more! They realized they had been wrong and had suffered for it, but now God had brought them back to the land. How wonderful!

It's true they were a small nation and still under the rule of another. But they were in the land, worshiping the God who placed them there according to His promises. In His city and with the Temple ready, they were anticipating the coming of Messiah, the Son of David, who would deliver them once and for all.

Ezra, a priest, and Nehemiah, the king of Persia's cupbearer, returned to Jerusalem to rebuild the broken and burned city walls and to lead a spiritual revival among the people.

Four Hundred Years of Anticipation

Four hundred years—that's a long time in anyone's book. But it is especially long when you are waiting for something or someone. Since the time of Nehemiah, the Jewish nation had been anticipating the Messiah of whom Ezekiel had spoken who would end their oppression. They were waiting for God to appoint a king from David's line to shepherd His people. But during these 400 years the Lord God seemingly kept silent. It's true, God did not communicate through prophets during this time, but He was working. Things were happening.

Back in 603 B.C. God enabled Daniel to interpret the dream God gave King Nebuchadnezzar and predict the rise and fall of nations and the transfer of global power. During these 400 years God was making the dream vision come true.

Nebuchadnezzar's glorious kingdom (represented by the gold head) was short-lived just as Daniel predicted. Cyrus, king of Persia, was conquering kingdom after kingdom and amassing a huge army. The city of Babylon eluded capture because of its enormous walls built on either side of the Euphrates River which flowed through the city. In 539 B.C. Cyrus diverted the flow of the river into irrigation channels and thus marched under the walls by means of a road created by the dried-up river, defeating Babylon's last king, Belshazzar.

The Medo-Persian Empire (represented by the silver chest and arms) then lasted much longer—over 200 years—but when 22-year-old Alexander of Greece met Darius of Persia on the battlefield of Gaugamela, that changed. Desiring to use his much feared scythe-wheeled chariots and his massive army of more than 200,000[16]

to conquer Alexander, Darius chose this flat field and had his men plow and level it to his advantage. But when Alexander arrived and assessed the situation, he turned to the right, luring foolish Darius into rough, rocky territory. Alexander's victory marked the end of Persian rule.

Eleven years later at only 33 years of age while ruling the largest empire of the ancient world, Alexander died. Although his life was short, the Greek Empire he founded (represented by the bronze belly and thighs), continued for over 250 years divided into four independently ruled regions. Ptolemy's dynasty (in Egypt) lasted the longest but finally came to an end when Cleopatra committed suicide under house arrest by Octavian of Rome.

When Octavian returned to Rome, he was declared "principal citizen," becoming the first emperor of the Roman Empire (represented by the iron legs and feet of iron and ceramic). Octavian was not referred to as king or dictator, but rather Augustus (the revered one), a name passed to succeeding emperors. Over the years several divisions of the empire took place, the final division being East and West in A.D. 395. The end of the Western Roman Empire is marked by Romulus Augustus' abdication of the throne before a Germanic general in 476.

During all these events and while rule over the Jews was being passed from one kingdom to another, the anticipation was building. As kingdoms rose and fell, the Jews couldn't help but wonder, "When would Messiah come to establish his kingdom (represented by the rock) which would last forever?"

---

16 Some estimates have Persia's army numbering one million at this time!

In the 400 years or so between the Old and New Testament eras, some major political, social, and religious developments occurred that influenced life in the New Testament era.

Birth of Jesus, the Christ

Isaiah the prophet declared, "Take note and be watching: A virgin will become pregnant and have a son. He will be called Emmanuel (Hebrew: God with us)." When the time was finally right in God's plan (more than 700 years later), He sent His messenger, Gabriel, to a village in Galilee. There he spoke with a young virgin who was promised in marriage to a man named Joseph. They were both descendants of King David.

"Hello, Special One!" Gabriel greeted her. "God be with you."

Mary was shocked and shaken.

"Don't be afraid, Mary. God is blessing you with a special baby! Call him Jesus."

He will be great; there is no other One
Who comes from the Most High; is truly God's Son.
To Him the Lord God will give David's throne.
On it He will sit and rule, He alone.
He'll rule Jacob's house, forever defend
His nation, His kingdom will never end.

Amazed and confused, Mary asked, "How will I have a baby? I've not had relations with a man."

"The Holy Spirit will come on you, blanketing you with the power of the Most High. So the One to whom you give birth will be called the holy Son of God … Nothing is impossible with God."

Joseph loved Mary. So when Mary started to show evidence of being pregnant before they were married, he wanted to cancel the wedding quietly so she wouldn't be open to ridicule.

But God sent an angel to him in a dream. "Joseph, descendant of David, go ahead and get married. It's true Mary is pregnant, but the child was conceived by God's Holy Spirit. I want you to name the son that will be born Jesus (Yahweh saves) because he will save his people from their sins."

When Joseph woke up, he did as he was told in the dream. He went ahead with his marriage to Mary and determined to name the baby Jesus.[17]

About that time, Caesar Augustus decreed: "Everyone must register in your hometown." So Joseph and Mary, being from David's line, left Nazareth in Galilee and went to Bethlehem (known as "The City of David") in Judea. They had trouble finding a place to stay and ended up making do with a feeding trough for a crib. While they were there, the baby came! Mary wrapped Him in strips of cloth and laid Him in a feeding trough.

That night shepherds were looking after their sheep in the field close by. Without warning, an angel from God showed up in blazing glory. The shepherds were paralyzed with fear!

"Don't be afraid," the angel told them. "I came to tell you of a great, joyous event everyone should know about: A Savior who will be Messiah and Master of all was born today in David's city. Look for a baby wrapped in cloths lying in a feeding trough."

Amazed, the shepherds said, "God has revealed something special to us. Let's get to Bethlehem now to see it." They ran to the town and found the baby in the feeding trough, Mary and Joseph at His side. Then they told everyone they met what the angel had told them about Jesus.

---

17 Even though Joseph married her right away, he waited to have sexual relations with her until after the baby conceived by the Holy Spirit was born.

At God's appointed time, He sent His Son to earth, born of a virgin named Mary, as the special King and Savior He had promised for centuries.

Family History of Jesus

Around 4,000 years ago God told an old man to leave his country and his family and move to an undisclosed place. God also promised this 75-year-old man with no children that He would make him famous, build a great nation of his **descendants**, give him all the **land** he would need for that nation, and use one of his descendants to **bring blessing to all peoples of the world**. Could that really happen?

It seemed impossible, but when Abraham was 100 years old, that promised son, Isaac, was born. We follow Abraham's **descendants** through Isaac and Jacob and others and find that by the time their family left Egypt, they were a nation of around two million people. Those people became the nation of Israel in the **land** God promised them, sometimes called Canaan, sometimes Palestine.

Around 3,000 years ago, one of Abraham's **descendants** named David became king of Israel. God reiterated the promise He made to Abraham, promising David that God would make him famous, give Israel their **land** once and for all, ensuring peace, and that his **descendants** would reign forever on David's throne.

A few years later the nation was divided. Then the northern half, Israel, was taken captive, dispersed throughout Assyria, and never heard from again. After that, the southern kingdom, Judah, went into exile in Babylon, returning to the **land** 70 years later, broken but hopeful.

The Jews remembered the promises. They heard more and more predictions and promises of one who would come to save them. He would come from David's line. Genealogies[18] became extremely important to the Jewish people as they wondered who would be the one to deliver them and establish their land forever. "Son of David" became a crucial title for the one who would come to be the Messiah, Savior, Deliverer.

So genealogies were kept carefully. Linear genealogies traced a person's lineage from son to father to grandfather, etc., citing only one person per generation. Closed linear genealogies include every generation. Open linear genealogies leave one or more generations out, but follow the single familial path. Horizontal genealogies include several or all of the sons of a father side by side (thus the term "horizontal") in the list. The Bible includes all three types of genealogies.

Around 2,000 years ago Jesus was born. One man (Matthew) traced His genealogy back to David and Abraham through Joseph, the one assumed[19] to be His father. Matthew linked Jesus to David, showing His legal connection to royalty. Could Jesus be the One spoken of by Isaiah, "born of a virgin"? Matthew mentions Mary while others don't.

Another historian (Luke) traced Jesus' line all the way back to Adam, showing His humanity. Could He be the Satan Conqueror God promised to Adam and Eve so long ago—the One who would deal with the sin issue once and for all—**blessing** all the peoples of the world like no one has ever or could ever bless them? Jesus' extraordinary pedigree qualifies Him to fulfill these prophecies and so many more.

The genealogical records of Jesus connect Him to several prominent Old Testament people, including Abraham and King David, which made Jesus eligible to be the Savior and King that God had promised.

---

18 Genealogy: A record or account of the ancestry and descent of a person, family, group, etc. (Dictionary.com).
19 Although Joseph was Jesus' legal father, in "Birth of Jesus Christ" we already learned that Jesus was conceived by the Holy Spirit of God.

NEW
TESTAMENT

ANTICIPATION

ARRIVAL

SECLUSION

POPULARITY

OPPOSITION

SUFFERING

VICTORY

APOSTLES

CHURCH

TRIBULATION

KINGDOM

JUDGMENT

RESTORATION

Early Events in Jesus' Life

Forty days had flown by! Joseph and Mary had obediently circumcised their son eight days after He was born and named him Jesus. Now, they had to get to the Temple in Jerusalem and present Jesus—their firstborn male child—to the Lord according to Leviticus 12. The Law required a sacrifice of a lamb, a pair of turtledoves, or two young pigeons. The birds were one-fifth the cost of a lamb so, far from home on a tight budget, Joseph prepared the birds while Mary got Jesus ready. Then they headed to the Temple.

Earlier, God had spoken to Simeon, a godly man living in prayerful anticipation of the Messiah. God revealed to him that he would see God's chosen One before he died. The Spirit led him to the Temple again on Jesus' dedication day.

When Joseph and Mary arrived with 40-day-old Jesus, Simeon was waiting for them. To their amazement, Simeon took Jesus in his arms and praised God: "Sovereign Lord, bring me home in peace, for these old eyes of mine have seen your salvation just as you promised. I see You want everyone to know that this One will be a God-revealing light for all nations as He glorifies your people Israel."

The couple was astonished! Jesus was conceived by the Holy Spirit; they already knew He was unique, but they were seeing and hearing more evidence of His uniqueness. As Simeon returned the baby and blessed them, they may have thought back to when the shepherds came looking for the Savior. They may have remembered Isaiah's prophecy: "Those walking in darkness will see a great light; those living in a dark land will have the light shine on them." Maybe they recalled Solomon's dedication of the Temple when he prayed that "all the peoples of the earth" would know God. As time passed, they would encounter more amazing proofs of Jesus' uniqueness.

One day a lavish entourage came to town, their camels loaded with treasure. The town buzzed with the news. Who were these men? What were they doing here in this forgotten corner of the world? Rich, dignified, these were respected sages from far away in the East. They came directly to Joseph and Mary's house. They explained how a star led them first to Jerusalem, then to Bethlehem. They told how they had stopped in Jerusalem, looking for the king who had been born and how the scribes, called in by King Herod, told them about the prophecy that God's shepherd for Israel would be born in lowly Bethlehem. They worshiped Jesus and gave him gold, expensive perfume, and spices—kingly gifts.

The surprises continued: after the Easterners left, an angel appeared to Joseph again saying, "Get up, take the child and Mary and run to Egypt! Stay there until I tell you, because Herod is going to search for Jesus so he can kill Him."

As they headed for Egypt, they had to be astonished, not only at the amazing events they had seen these past two years, but also at God's faithful care and provision. Not long ago they were so poor they couldn't move back to their hometown after the census and had to offer pigeons instead of a lamb. But now they were able to travel to Egypt because strangers from the East brought Jesus gifts.

Years later, when Jesus was 12, His parents thought they lost Him on their way home from a Passover trip to Jerusalem.

Frantic, they went back to Jerusalem. Three days later they found Jesus in the Temple conversing with the teachers. "Why did you do this to us? We've been looking all over for you, worried sick."

"Why?" Jesus answered. "You didn't realize I needed to be in my Father's house?" They did not understand, but as they returned to Nazareth with their submissive son, Mary kept thinking about these evidences of Jesus' uniqueness.

As he grew up, Jesus' wisdom became more evident and everyone liked him. More importantly, he honored God.

Some early events in the life of Jesus, as a baby and as a young boy, marked Him as a special person who would later bring hope and peace to multitudes of people.

Temptations by Satan

Long ago, Lucifer, that most beautiful of angels, became proud and wanted to be like God. God cast him out of Heaven and he became known as Satan (adversary) and the Devil (accuser).

In the garden he took the form of a serpent and tempted Eve to disobey. God judged him and promised to send one who would defeat him once and for all. Adam and Eve and many of their descendants have waited for that one to come.

Meanwhile, Satan continued to be powerful and had the freedom to tempt and accuse people through the centuries. He went before God, trying to get his way, even challenging God. He tempted Job (a famous patriarch), King David, and others. Even though God allowed these circumstances, He rebuked Satan and protected His people from him. Satan knew Jesus was God's special promised One so he determined to disqualify Him by tempting Him to sin.

Jesus had come down from Nazareth in Galilee to the Jordan River where He was baptized by John. As soon as Jesus came out of the water He saw the heavens torn apart! Out came the Spirit and a voice. The Spirit looked like a dove descending on Jesus. The voice said: "I am pleased with You, my dearly loved Son."

That's when it began. The Spirit, controlling Jesus, led Him into the desert to be tempted by Satan for 40 days. Jesus fasted the entire time. At the end of 40 days he was famished. Satan saw an opportunity. He would tempt Jesus at a moment of weakness.

"You must be hungry. Since You're God's Son, make bread out of these stones." Jesus is God's Son, God had said so at His baptism.

Satan was tempting Jesus to work outside the purpose of His service: to use His power for self, acting independently of God's plan.

Jesus answered, "God's Word says, 'It takes more than mere bread to sustain man's life.'"

Satan took Jesus and gave Him a glimpse of all the kingdoms of the world at once. He said, "I will give you authority over all this and the glory that goes with it. It is at my disposal to give to whomever I wish. Just worship me and all this can be yours." God had said He was pleased with His Son. Satan was attempting to disqualify Jesus so He would be "displeased."

But Jesus answered, "God's Word says, 'Worship and serve the Lord God alone.'"

Finally, Satan took Jesus to the top of the Temple in Jerusalem and said, "If You are God's Son, jump! The Bible says that God will protect His own with angels; even keep Him from stubbing His toe."

Jesus had had enough. "God's Word says, 'Do not test the Lord your God.'"

Satan was finished. Since he had no more with which to tempt Jesus, he left Him until another opportunity arose.

Jesus was victorious. Where Adam and Eve, their children, and Israel failed in similar temptations, Jesus passed the test, always responding with God's Word. God showed Satan (and us) that Jesus couldn't fall; He wouldn't fail. He is God's Son, the One sent to defeat Satan. Satan was defeated!

After being baptized by John the Baptist, Jesus was personally tempted by Satan, but He resisted Satan's temptations with statements from God's Word in the Old Testament.

John the Baptist's Testimony

Even though Jesus grew up in an obscure town, supposedly the son of a simple carpenter, there were indications that He was special, that He was the unique God-sent Messiah. A few years after His death a man would write that He existed with God before time began, that He was actually the Creator God who gives life to men, lights their way, and overpowers darkness. This man saw Jesus as God taking on a human body and coming to earth to live with mankind.

Centuries earlier, the LORD God sought to be with His people Israel in the desert and His glory shone through the cloud and the fire. Now He had come in human form to truly live with people and some saw His glory as the unique Son of God overflowing with grace and truth. But many—even His own people—did not recognize Him for who He was.

One man did recognize Him and proclaimed it to others. His name was John. God sent John for this very purpose: to be a witness that Jesus was the light that overpowers the darkness. But John didn't always know who Jesus was. He had an unusual experience that convinced him.

One day John was in Bethany on the east side of the Jordan River talking with some priests who had been sent by the Jewish leaders to question him. Among other things, he said, "One is coming after me who is better than I because He existed before me."

"Are you the Messiah?"

"No."

"Then are you Elijah returning to us before the day of the Lord as Malachi prophesied?"

"I am not."

"Are you 'The Prophet' Moses told our fathers about?"

"No."

"Well then, who? We need an answer for those who sent us! Who are you?"

"I am the one Isaiah spoke of when he declared that there would be a voice crying out in the desert, 'Prepare the way of the Lord.'"

The next day Jesus approached John. When John saw Him, he lifted his voice, "Look! Here is the Lamb of God who takes away the sin of the world! He is the One I spoke of when I said 'One is coming after me who is better than I because He existed before me.' Even though my purpose in baptizing with water was to reveal the Messiah to Israel, I hadn't recognized Jesus as He. But after I baptized Him, I saw the Spirit come down out of Heaven in the form of a dove and remain on Him. I still may not have realized the significance of this event, but the One who sent me to baptize with water told me, 'He on whom you see the Spirit descend and remain is the One who baptizes with the Holy Spirit.' Listen! With my own eyes I have seen it. I can testify without a doubt to you: This is the Son of God."

God had promised through Ezekiel that He would put His Spirit in mankind. The Day of Atonement was to take away Israel's sins. Now John was saying that Jesus would baptize with the Holy Spirit and take away the sins not only of Israel, but of the whole world. Simeon saw Him as the light that Isaiah had previously predicted. This Jesus was special!

After Jesus resisted Satan's temptations, John the Baptist boldly announced that Jesus was the special King and Savior, God's Lamb, who would take away the sin of the world.

The Selection of Jesus' Disciples

The day after John's amazing declaration of Jesus as the Lamb of God, John was with two of his followers. He saw Jesus walking by, and said, "Here He is, God's special Lamb."

On hearing these words, John's two followers spent the day with Jesus. Andrew was one of the two. He was so impressed that the first thing he did was to find his brother, Simon, and bring him to Jesus. "We've found the Messiah!"

Jesus took one look at him and said, "You're John's son, Simon? I'm going to call you Cephas" (or Peter, which means "Rock").

The next day Jesus decided to go to Galilee. When He got there, He ran across Philip and said, "Come, follow Me." (Philip's hometown was Bethsaida, the same as Andrew and Peter.)

Philip went and found Nathanael and told him, "We've found the One Moses wrote of in the Law, the One foretold by the prophets. It's Jesus, Joseph's son, the one from Nazareth!" Nathanael said, "Nazareth? You've got to be kidding."

But Philip said, "Come, see for yourself."

When Jesus saw him coming, He said, "There's a real Israelite, not a false bone in his body."

Nathanael said, "Where did you get that idea? You don't know me."

Jesus answered, "One day, long before Philip called you here, I saw you under the fig tree."

Nathanael exclaimed, "Rabbi! You are the Son of God, the King of Israel!"

Jesus said, "You've become a believer simply because I say I saw you one day sitting under the fig tree? You haven't seen anything yet! Before this is over you're going to see Heaven open and God's angels descending to the Son of Man and ascending again."

Jesus had many followers, but we're not told the stories of how Jesus met all of them. We do know that as He visited some of them where they worked He began to call on them to follow Him in a special way. He called James, John, Peter, and Andrew from their fishing boats by the Sea of Galilee. He called Matthew from his tax collector's booth in the city.

Then, one evening Jesus climbed a mountain by Himself. He stayed on the mountain all night praying. When He came down the next morning Jesus chose 12 of His followers and designated them apostles (sent ones): Peter, Andrew, James, John, Philip, Bartholomew, Matthew, Thomas, James (Alphaeus' son), Simon (nicknamed the Zealot), Judas (James' son), and Judas Iscariot (who would eventually betray him).

Later, somewhere in the Galilee region, Jesus called the 12 together, gave them power and authority over demons and diseases, and sent them out to proclaim God's kingdom and to heal. The apostles visited villages all around, preaching the good news everywhere they went.

From among His committed followers, Jesus chose a special group of disciples that were often referred to as "apostles" or simply, "the Twelve."

Encounter with a Religious Leader

The Passover, the highlight of the Jewish calendar, had come and Nicodemus should have been pleased and excited. After all, this would be one more opportunity to secure his good standing with God—and he was well on his way. He believed, as all good Pharisees did, that the two requirements for God's acceptance were to be born into a Jewish family (or convert to Judaism) and to keep the Law and traditions. He was not only a Jew, but as part of the Sanhedrin, he was a ruler of the Jews! And Passover—one more chance to gain favor with God—had arrived. So why was he troubled?

It was this new teacher, Jesus. Nicodemus was intrigued by Him. Could He be the Messiah? But some things just didn't seem to make sense, like when his colleagues asked Jesus for a sign. Jesus' answer was confusing: "Destroy this temple, and in three days I will raise it up." Nicodemus had watched the building of the Temple for 46 years—nearly his entire life—and this man would raise it in three days?

People flocked to Him at the Passover Feast, "believing" in Him because of His miracles. And yet Jesus remained aloof. It's as if He could see their hearts, as if He knew they were simply amazed at the signs but were not truly placing their trust in Him.

Nicodemus had to see Jesus; he had to have his questions answered: Are you the Messiah? Are we missing something? How does one truly get into the kingdom of God? But he couldn't be seen with Jesus, not as a member of the Sanhedrin. So he met Jesus at night.

"Teacher, we know that You come from God or else You couldn't do these signs."

Even though Nicodemus didn't ask the questions rolling around in his mind, Jesus addressed them.

"This is the truth: to see God's kingdom, you need to experience a second birth."

"How can I, a grown man, get into my mother's womb again to be born?"

Nicodemus was still caught up with the belief that he had to be physically born into a Jewish family, to be connected through the Mosaic Covenant. But Jesus was talking about the New Covenant, about God giving mankind a new heart and a new spirit. Nicodemus didn't get it.

Jesus continued. "Even you, a teacher of Israel, don't understand these things. People only talk about what they know, they tell others what they see and understand. I know what I'm talking about, but you people don't believe Me. I explain heavenly truths with earthly illustrations and you don't understand. What else can I do?

"I have come from Heaven to make this truth clear: just like Moses lifted up the serpent in the desert, so the Son of Man must be lifted up so that those who believe in Him may live. God loved the world so much that He gave His unique Son so that those who believe won't be lost, but will have eternal life. God didn't send His Son into the world to condemn people; He sent Him to save them through Him. But while anyone who does not believe is already condemned, those who believe are saved from condemnation."

That night Nicodemus learned that it is not physical birth or keeping the Law that guarantees entrance into God's kingdom. Instead, he needed to believe what God said about the One lifted up, to look and be delivered from certain death, and to look to the One who could give him a new heart and a new spirit.

On one occasion, Jesus told Nicodemus, a prominent religious leader, that he needed to experience a spiritual birth in order to enter God's kingdom.

Encounter with a Samaritan Woman

One day Jesus went from Judea to Galilee. To make this trip Jews normally crossed the Jordan, traveled north, then crossed the Jordan again to arrive in Galilee. In this way they avoided Samaria. Their dislike for Samaritans went back several centuries. In 722 B.C., Assyria took Israel into captivity and brought polytheistic Babylonians to populate the land. Some of them converted to Judaism and anticipated "The Prophet" Moses foretold, but they didn't follow the entire Old Testament, so they rejected the idea that he would be from David's line. They built their own temple on Mt. Gerazim which was later destroyed, but some of them still worshiped on that mountain. These differences created hostility between Jews and Samaritans.

But Jesus loved all people. He didn't let prejudices affect His actions. He was determined to go through Samaria on this day to reach Galilee. About noon, tired from the trip, He stopped in Sychar and sat by a well Jacob had dug many years ago. A woman from the town, one of the despised Samaritans, came to draw water. Jesus asked her for a drink.

The woman responded. "You, a Jew, are asking for a drink from me, a Samaritan?"

Jesus answered. "If you understood who it is asking for a drink and what He has to offer, you would have asked and He would have given you living water."

"How, sir? You have nothing with which to draw water from this deep well. Certainly You are not greater than our father Jacob who gave us this well! He drank from it and provided water for his family and livestock."

"Everyone who drinks water from this well will be thirsty again, but those who drink from the water I offer will have their thirst quenched forever. The water I give will become a fountain of water springing up to eternal life."

"Oh, give me some of that water! Then I will never be thirsty or have to come here to draw water."

"Go get your husband."

"I have no husband."

Jesus responded, "Good answer. You've been married five times, and you are living with someone now."

"Sir, you must be a prophet from Israel. Our ancestors worshiped here on this mountain, but your people say all must worship in Jerusalem."

"Listen, woman, the time is coming when the Father will be worshiped neither here nor in Jerusalem. Your people worship in ignorance, but we worship the God we know will bring salvation through the Jews. Soon, even now, true worshipers will worship the Father in spirit and truth. Those are the type of worshipers God seeks, for He is spirit, and those who would worship Him must worship in spirit and truth."

The woman said, "I know Messiah, the One called Christ, will tell all about these things when He comes."

Jesus simply stated, "I am He."

The woman left her jar and ran to town, calling out, "Come, see a man who was able to tell me everything about myself. Could He be the Christ?"

People came to Jesus at the well. Many Samaritans from Sychar believed in Jesus because of the woman's story. They asked Jesus to stay, so He did for two days, and many more believed. Then they told the woman, "We no longer believe because of what you said. We heard Jesus ourselves and know without a doubt that He is the Savior of the world."

On another occasion, Jesus explained to a woman from Samaria how God could permanently satisfy her spiritual thirst.

Spread of Jesus' Fame

When Jesus returned to Galilee filled with the Holy Spirit, people all over that region began talking about Him. As He spoke in the synagogues, everyone enjoyed and spoke highly of His teaching.

At this time Jesus moved from His hometown, Nazareth, to Capernaum, nestled at the base of the Zebulun and Naphtali hills on the edge of the Sea of Galilee. (Isaiah's prophecy about "people living in darkness seeing a great light" was fulfilled as Jesus taught here.)

Jesus officially called four fishermen (Peter, Andrew, James, and John) who had been learning from Him to be His followers while in this region. Then He continued to teach about God's kingdom all over Galilee and He healed people of their diseases. Jesus' fame got around the entire Roman province of Syria, so people brought their sick (mentally, emotionally, physically, and spiritually); Jesus healed all of them! The more He healed, the more people came. They came from Galilee at first. But then crowds started coming from the "Ten Towns" on the other side of the lake, and all the way from Jerusalem and Judea, and from Perea on the other side of the Jordan River.

After this He went back to Nazareth (His hometown). Just like every other Sabbath, He went to the meeting place. He stood to read and was given an Isaiah scroll. Unrolling it, He found this well-known prophecy about the coming of Messiah: "God's Spirit is on Me. He chose Me to preach good news to the poor, to announce pardon to prisoners and recovery of sight to the blind, to set the burdened and battered free and to announce, 'This is God's year to act!'"

Every eye in the place watched Him intently as He rolled up the scroll, returned it to the assistant, and sat down to teach. Then He said, "This Scripture was fulfilled as you listened."

Everyone there was surprised at His speaking ability. "Isn't this Joseph's son, the one we've known since He was a boy?" "How did He get so wise all of a sudden?" "He's just a carpenter—Mary's boy." "His brothers are James, Justus, Jude, and Simon. Who does He think He is?" The little they knew about Him kept them from seeing the big picture and they became offended.

Jesus responded: "Of course you're going to quote the proverb, 'Doctor, heal yourself. We heard you did great miracles in Capernaum. Do them here in your hometown.' Well, it's true: No prophet is ever welcomed in his hometown. You must know there were plenty of widows in Israel during those three and a half years of drought and famine, but the only widow to whom Elijah was sent was in Zaraphath in Sidon. And there were plenty of lepers in Israel during Elisha's time, but the only one cleansed was Naaman the Syrian."

That made them angry. They threw Him out of the synagogue and out of the village. They took Him to a cliff so they could throw Him off, but He slipped right through their hands and headed to Capernaum where He taught the people on the Sabbath. Again, people were amazed, impressed with His clear, confident, authoritative teaching.

A demon-possessed man yelled, "Hey! Why are You here, Jesus, Nazarene? Are you here to destroy us? I know You are the Holy One of God. Why have You come?"

Jesus rebuffed him: "That's enough! Let the man go!" Right in front of the crowd the demon threw the man down and left without hurting him. If they weren't amazed before, they were now.

"What's this? Someone with such power and authority that He casts out demons with His word?"

Everyone was talking about Jesus in the entire area and the news spread like wildfire.

During the second year of His ministry, the crowds that were attracted to Jesus grew increasingly large, especially as He moved about the region around the Sea of Galilee.

Jesus' Power over a Stormy Sea

Several of Jesus' followers made their living as fishermen on the Sea of Galilee, a freshwater lake that is part of the Jordan River system. This below-sea-level lake, surrounded by hills, experiences abrupt temperature shifts and violent storms when clouds dive from the sheer cliffs down on to the lake.

One day, late in the afternoon, Jesus invited His followers to make the 10-kilometer trip across to the other side of the lake. So they clambered into a boat and started out. Other boats joined them. A huge storm developed quickly. Water poured into the boat as waves washed over them. The boat was sinking!

Where was Jesus? In the stern, sleeping soundly on a pillow! His followers shook Him. "Teacher, we're dying! Don't You care?"

Jesus woke up and spoke sternly to the wind and water: "Hush! Calm down!" It was as if the wind ran out of breath! The lake became like glass! Then Jesus turned to His followers.

"What's wrong? You're afraid? Don't you have any faith?"

They were awestruck, dumbfounded. "Who is this man? He speaks and the wind and water listen!"

On another evening when quite possibly the clouds could be seen forming over the hills, Jesus insisted that His followers get in the boat and go on ahead of Him to the other side while He dismissed a crowd. When the last person had left, Jesus climbed the mountain so He could be alone to pray. He prayed late into the night.

While He was praying, His followers in the boat had gotten far from land, and the wind and waves were beating against them. Early in the morning while it was still dark, Jesus walked on the water right up to them. This scared them more than the storm. "A ghost!"

Jesus wasted no time in comforting them. "It's okay; it is I, Jesus. No need to fear."

Peter gained some courage. "Master, if it's really You, help me walk on the water, too."

"Okay. Come on."

Peter went over the side and actually walked on the water toward Jesus! But as he walked he started noticing the tempestuous wind and waves and lost his courage. He started to sink and cried for help. "Save me, Master!"

In an instant Jesus grabbed him. Then He said, "You don't have much faith! You were doing well; why did you doubt?"

They both climbed into the boat, and the wind stopped. Jesus' followers had watched the whole thing and now they worshiped Jesus. "Now we know for sure! You are God's Son!"

This was the very first time any of Jesus' followers called Jesus God's Son. They had seen Jesus perform many miracles before, but these experienced fishermen who were accustomed to storms on this lake, had been terrified by these storms. But when Jesus came along walking on that tumultuous, terrifying, seemingly out-of-control sea, He showed them that He was in control. They saw that Jesus was definitely more powerful than nature. He was supernatural. They may have been thinking of Psalm 89 which attributes the ruling of the oceans and the subduing of storm-tossed waves to God. Or maybe they thought of Psalm 107 which tells the story of sailors crying for help and God stilling the waves to a whisper. Jesus was doing things that only God could do.

Jesus' followers were beginning to understand how He could control the laws of nature. Later one of them wrote this about Him: He "was God … everything was created through Him; not one thing came into being without Him."

Jesus even amazed His closest disciples by calming the Sea of Galilee, when its raging, stormy waters threatened to overwhelm their boat.

Jesus' Power over a Legion of Demons

After the storm ended, they sailed on to Gerasene country, on the east side of the lake, opposite Galilee. A man tormented by demons lived in a cemetery there. He hadn't worn clothes or lived in his home for quite a while. Many times the demons threw the man into convulsions. The people tried to restrain him, securing him with chains and handcuffs, but the demons drove him crazy and he broke free over and over.

When Jesus stepped out of the boat, this madman met Him. Jesus started to order the demons from him, the man screamed, then fell to his knees.

"What business do we have between us? You're Jesus, Son of the Most High God! Please don't punish me!"

"State your name."

"Legion." Just as "legion" was used for a body of thousands of Roman soldiers, so they were called legion because many demons tormented this man. They pleaded with Jesus not to order them into the abyss, the eternal fire prepared for the devil and his demons.

A large herd of pigs was feeding on a nearby hill. The demons begged Jesus for permission to enter the pigs. Jesus allowed it. The demons left the man and entered the pigs, which stampeded over a cliff into the lake and drowned.

The ones who were tending the pigs saw it all. They ran off, telling the story to everyone—city and country dwellers alike. So people went out to see what had happened. They found Jesus and at His feet, the man—formerly demon-possessed, naked and uncontrollable—sitting there dressed and acting quite normal! Those who had seen it happen told about his transformation.

The people realized that Jesus was more powerful than this demon-possessed man that they had not been able to control for years. That frightened them. So the majority of the people from the Gerasene countryside got together and asked Jesus to leave.

Jesus got back in the boat to head out. The man whom He had delivered from the demons begged to go along. Jesus refused. "Go back to your family and friends and tell them the great things God did in you." So he did. This transformed man proclaimed all over town the great things Jesus did in him.

Later, Jesus was teaching and knew the thoughts and challenged their thinking. "Civil war ruins nations. Constantly squabbling families fall to pieces. If Satan casts out demons, he defeats himself. You accuse Me of working with the Devil, the prince of demons, to cast out demons. But if that were the case, what about your own exorcists? How do they do it? But if I cast out demons through God's power, then know that God's kingdom is here.

"When a fully armed strong man guards his house, his property is safe. But if a stronger man with better weapons challenges him, he is in trouble. He had confidence in his armor, but it's gone along with his precious possessions.

"There is no neutral ground: If you're not on My side, you are My enemy; if you're not helping Me bring people to God, you're pushing them away.

"When a demon is cast out of someone, it is as if it wanders through the desert looking for an oasis: another unsuspecting soul it can possess. If it doesn't find anyone, it goes back to its old 'house.' Arriving there, it finds the person swept and in order. It then runs out and gathers seven more demons more evil than itself and they all take up residence. That person ends up far worse than if he'd never been freed from the demon in the first place."

On the eastern shore of the Sea of Galilee, Jesus cast many evil spirits out of a severely afflicted man, and his life was dramatically transformed in many ways.

Jesus' Claims of Oneness with God

Some people, like John the Baptist, noticed unique indications that Jesus was special. Some believed he was Messiah, specially sent from God. Others didn't.

One Sabbath Jesus visited the beautiful covered Bethesda Pool near the Sheep Gate in Jerusalem. Many blind, lame, and paralyzed people lay in the shelter around the pool. One of them had been an invalid for 38 years.

Jesus spoke to that man. "Get up, roll up your mat, and walk."

Immediately the man was healed. He rolled up his mat and walked around.

Jewish leaders saw the man carrying his mat on the Sabbath. They told him, "It is against the Law for you to carry your mat on the Sabbath."

Now it wasn't really against the Law that Moses had received from God. It was against the rabbinic interpretation of the Law that went far beyond the original intent, but the man who was healed didn't know the difference. He answered the Jews. "I'm just carrying my mat because the man who healed me told me to roll it up and walk."

"Who told you that?" they asked.

The man didn't know. A crowd had gathered and Jesus had slipped away. Later Jesus found him in the Temple. "Look how you can walk now! Live right so nothing worse happens to you."

Then the man went and told the Jewish leaders Jesus was the one who had healed him. The leaders had been persecuting Him for healing people on the Sabbath. Jesus told them, "Listen. My Father works every day and so do I." After that, the Jewish leaders wanted to kill Him even more. Not only for breaking the Sabbath, but because He called God His own Father and made Himself equal with God.

Another time the Jewish leaders were insulting Jesus. He answered them. "If anyone keeps My word, he will never see death."

"Now we know You are crazy! Abraham died along with all the prophets, but You say anyone who keeps Your word will not die. Are You greater than our ancestor Abraham, who died? And the prophets, who died? Who do You think You are?"

(Some of the Jewish teachers believed that Abraham could foresee Messiah's coming. Jesus probably alluded to that belief with His answer.) "Your ancestor Abraham rejoiced that he would see My day. He saw My coming and was glad."

"What? You are not even 50 years old, and You have seen Abraham?"

"Listen to Me: before Abraham was, I am."

The Jews considered this a blasphemous claim to be God which was punishable by stoning. So they picked up stones to throw at Jesus, but Jesus hid Himself and left the Temple.

Later, during Hanukkah, Jesus was walking in the Temple. The Jewish leaders gathered around and asked, "How long will you keep us in suspense? If You are the Christ, tell us in plain language."

"I told you, but you don't believe … I and the Father are one." Twice more that day they picked up stones to kill Him. They tried to seize Him, but He eluded their grasp.

Several times when Jesus declared that He was the Son of God and was one with His Father, some people were greatly offended and attempted to kill Him.

Jesus' Power over Blindness

Walking down the street one Sabbath, Jesus saw a man blind from birth. His followers wanted to know who was to blame—his parents or the man himself—but Jesus simply wanted to show what God could do in the man's life. He spit in the dust, made clay with the saliva, rubbed the clay on the blind man's eyes, and said, "Go, wash at Siloam Pool." The man went and washed—and saw!

Everyone was talking about it—the man's relatives, neighbors—all who had seen him begging for years. "Hey, isn't this the blind beggar?" "It's him all right!"

Some doubted. "It's not the same man. It just looks like him."

He said, "It's me. It's really me!"

"How did your eyes get healed?"

"A man named Jesus made clay, rubbed it on my eyes, and told me, 'Go wash in Siloam.' I did, and now I see."

"So where is He?"

"I don't know."

They marched the man off to the Pharisees. The Pharisees grilled him again about how he had come to see. He said, "He put clay on my eyes, I washed, and now I see."

Some of the Pharisees said, "Obviously, this man can't be from God. He doesn't keep the Sabbath."

Others disagreed. "How can an evil man do miracles like this?" They were divided.

"So, man-born-blind, you were there. He healed you. What do you say about Him?"

"He is a prophet."

The Jewish leaders didn't believe the man was blind to begin with. So they called his parents. "Is this your son, the one you say was born blind? What happened that he sees now?"

The Jewish leaders had decided that anyone who declared Jesus to be the Messiah would be excommunicated from the synagogue. So his parents avoided responding directly to their question. "Oh, he's our son, and he definitely was born blind. But how should we know who healed him? Ask him. He's a grown man; he can speak for himself."

The leaders called the man who was born blind back. "Be honest before God. We know this man is an impostor."

"I don't know about that. But one thing I know for sure: I was blind … now I can see."

"What did He do to you? How did He heal you?"

"I told you before, but you didn't listen. Why do you want to hear it again? Are you eager to follow Him?"

Now they were upset. "Maybe you follow Him, but we follow Moses. We know for sure that Moses was God's spokesman, but we don't even know where this man comes from."

"This is amazing! If anyone is from God, it is the One who heals a man born blind—something no one has ever done. Yet you religious leaders say you don't know anything about the One who healed me—a man blind from birth! Surely you see He is unique and not a common sinner."

The leaders threw him out. "You are nobody! How dare you take that tone with us!"

Jesus heard the leaders had thrown him out and went to him. "Do you believe in the Son of Man?"

"Show Him to me, sir, and I will believe."

Jesus said, "You're looking at Him. Don't you recognize My voice?"

"Master, I believe," the man said, and worshiped Him.

In an unprecedented act, Jesus healed a man who was born blind, which shocked the man's parents and neighbors, offended the religious leaders, and resulted in the man's sincere faith response.

Stories of God's Love and Forgiveness

As Jesus traveled around Galilee and Judea, He told more than 50 parables.[20] Sometimes they were hard to understand, sometimes easy. One day, He told these easy-to-understand stories among others.

"A man had two sons. His younger son spoke to him. 'Father, I want my inheritance right now.'

"So the father divided the property between them. Soon the younger son packed his bags and left for a faraway land where he quickly wasted all he had. When he was out of money, that country suffered a drought which made food scarce for everyone, including him. He started to work for someone there, slopping pigs out in the fields. He was so hungry he would have eaten the pig slop, but no one gave him any.

"Then he came to his senses. He said, 'The farmhands that work for my father have plenty to eat while I'm starving to death. I'm getting up out of this mess and going back to my father. I'll tell him I have sinned against God and against him; and that I don't deserve to be called his son. I'll ask him to take me on as a hired hand.' So he got up and started home.

"While still a long way off, the father saw his son. Filled with love, he ran to, embraced, and kissed him. The son began the speech he had planned: 'Father, I have sinned against God and against you; I don't deserve to be called your son—'

"Ignoring the speech, the father called to his servants, 'Quick. Bring the finest clothes we have and dress him, including a ring for his finger and sandals for his feet. Then prepare a special meal with one of the calves we are raising. We're going to feast and celebrate because my son is here who I thought was dead, but is truly alive! He was hopelessly lost and now is found!' So they began the party.

"Meanwhile his older son was working in the field. At quitting time he came in. Approaching the house, he heard music and dancing. 'What's going on?' he asked a houseboy. 'Your brother is back! Your father ordered a big party with roast beef to celebrate his safe return.'

"This upset the older brother; he refused to join the party. His father came out and tried to talk to him, to no avail.

"'I faithfully served you all these years without creating a single problem, but you never threw a party for me and my friends! But this son of yours who squandered your money on prostitutes shows up and you go all out!'

"'No, no, dear son, you don't get it. I'm so glad you're always with me, and everything I have is yours. But it is only right to celebrate this happy day. Your brother was dead, and now he's alive! He was lost, but now he's found!'"

Jesus told another story to some who had confidence in their own moral performance and scorned others:

"A Pharisee and a tax collector went up to the Temple to pray. The Pharisee stood alone and prayed like this: 'Oh, God, I thank you that I am not a sinner like other people—thieves, cheats, adulterers—and especially like this tax collector. I fast twice a week and I give 10 percent of my income.'

"In contrast, the tax collector, hidden in the shadows, head bowed in shame, beating on his chest, said, 'God, I beg for mercy. I'm a sinner in need of forgiveness.'

"Understand this: The tax collector, not the Pharisee, went home right with God. Those who lift themselves up in pride will be humbled, but the one who humbles himself will be lifted up."

---

20 Parable: a simple story that illustrates an important truth ("little story, big truth").

Jesus used many parables in His teaching, but one of the most famous was about a wayward son whom his father forgave and a selfish brother who didn't understand.

Jesus' Teaching about Hell

Jesus healed many people as He moved around Palestine. He claimed to be God on several occasions. He preached about God's love and forgiveness. But He also taught about Hell more than anyone else in the Bible. As God's Son, He understood the realities of Hell more than anyone could and loved people more than anyone else. One day, after telling several stories about God's love and forgiveness, Jesus told this story:

"A rich man wore the finest clothes money could buy and ate like a king every day. Living in the street outside the walls of the rich man's mansion a poor beggar named Lazarus lay covered with sores. As the dogs licked at his sores he hoped to eat at least whatever fell from the rich man's table.

"When the poor man died, angels carried him to Abraham's side. The rich man also died and was buried.

"From Hell, in constant torment, the rich man looked and saw Abraham and Lazarus far away. He cried out, 'Father Abraham, have mercy on me! Let Lazarus dip the tip of his finger in water and come cool my tongue. I am in agony in these flames!'

"Abraham answered. 'Child, don't you remember that while you lived, you had everything you needed and Lazarus suffered hard times? Now he is comforted here and you are in agony. But even if someone from here wanted to go there or if someone there wanted to come here, it is impossible because a cavernous, impassable gulf is established between us.'

"Still in anguish, the rich man pleaded for his family: 'Then please, send Lazarus to warn my five brothers so they can escape this impending doom.' Abraham answered, 'The Word of God gives clear warning. Let them heed it.'

"'But, Father Abraham,' the rich man continued, 'If someone comes back from the dead to warn them, they will repent.'

"'No,' responded Abraham, 'if they aren't convinced by God's Word, then they won't be convinced by someone coming back from the dead.'"

Jesus spoke of this future place of torment many times and in vivid detail. He spoke of darkness; weeping; gnashing of teeth; an unquenchable, eternal fire; and where the worm does not die.

Southwest of Jerusalem sat a perpetually burning, maggot-infested garbage dump which was previously a place where pagans and Jews alike offered infant sacrifices. By this time in history the Jews had been using this place as a picture of eternal punishment. Jesus also used this well-known Valley of Gehenna as a stark illustration of Hell. He spoke with conviction of Hell's reality and encouraged people to repent to avoid going there.

As He moved among the people, Jesus often lovingly but sternly warned them of the reality of eternal punishment in Hell and the urgent need to escape it.

Jesus' Power over Death

Lazarus, Mary, and Martha, a brother and sisters living in Bethany, were good friends of Jesus whom He loved very much. Lazarus became ill, so his sisters sent a message to Jesus: "Lord, one whom You love is sick." Jesus told the messenger, "Don't worry, this illness will not leave Lazarus dead, but will glorify God as He glorifies His Son through this event." So Jesus stayed where He was two more days after He received the message. Then He said to the disciples, "It's time to go to Judea. Our friend, Lazarus, sleeps now but I will wake him up."

"Lord, if he is able to rest, he must be getting better!" His disciples responded. But Jesus had used the word "sleep" figuratively of his death. Now He explained: "Lazarus is dead. For your sake I am glad I was not there, so you may believe. Let's go to him now."

By the time Jesus arrived, Lazarus had been dead and buried four days and many Jews from Jerusalem (only three kilometers away) were present trying to console the sisters. When Martha heard Jesus was close, she ran to Him and said, "Master, if only You had been here, my brother would not have died. But I am convinced that whatever You ask of God, He will grant it."

"Your brother will rise again," Jesus told her.

"I know he will rise in the resurrection on the last day," Martha replied.

Jesus stated, "I am the resurrection and the life. Anyone who believes in Me will live, even if he dies. Everyone who lives and believes in Me will never die. Do you believe?"

Martha responded, "Yes, Master; I believe that You are the Christ, the Son of God, sent into the world." Then she left to get Mary. "The Teacher has arrived and is asking for you." Mary came and fell at Jesus' feet and also said, "Master, if You had been here, my brother would not have died."

Jesus was quite disturbed when He saw her crying and the Jews with her crying, too. "Where have you laid him?"

"Master, come and see," they replied.

Jesus was deeply affected and cried with them. When He reached the tomb, Jesus said, "Move the stone."

Martha interjected, "But Master, it's been four days. I'm sure there will be a strong odor."

But Jesus insisted, "Didn't I tell your messenger that if you believed, you would see God glorified in this?"

So they moved the stone. Then Jesus looked to Heaven and said, "Father, thank You for hearing Me as You always do. I am speaking aloud so that those standing here might believe that You sent Me." Then, focusing on the tomb, Jesus shouted, "Lazarus, come out here."

With hands and feet still bound in linen burial strips and face wrapped in a cloth, the one who had died came out!

Jesus told them, "Free him from those grave clothes."

When they saw what Jesus did, many Jews who had accompanied Mary believed in Jesus, but others went and told the Pharisees. So the leading priests and the Pharisees called the Council together. "What can we do now? Since this man performs notable miracles everyone will believe in Him, and the Romans will take away our position as leaders of the nation." From then on they made plans to kill Him.

But Jesus continued to travel about. Six days before the Passover, He returned to Bethany. Martha served a dinner and Lazarus, along with others, ate with Him. A large crowd came, not only to see Jesus, but Lazarus, too, since he had died and now lived. Now the leading priests planned to kill Lazarus also, because many Jews believed in Jesus after seeing and talking with Lazarus.

Jesus demonstrated His power over nature, demons, and physical infirmities, but perhaps His greatest miracle was bringing a dead man, who had been in the grave for four days, back to life.

Jesus' Triumphal Entry

Babylon, 539 B.C.

Octogenarian Daniel pours out his heart to God, baring his and his people Israel's sins, interceding for his city. While absorbed in his prayer during evening worship, the angel Gabriel swoops down to him like a bird out of Heaven. He tells Daniel that God heard his prayer and will send the Messiah. The extensive message included the following detail: 'Understand that from the time the word goes out to rebuild Jerusalem until the coming of the Anointed Leader, 490 years will pass." Less than 100 years later Artaxerxes permits Nehemiah to rebuild Jerusalem. At least one timetable puts the event told on this page 490 years later to the day.

Jerusalem, circa 520 B.C.

Zechariah declares and writes a message to Judah which becomes the Minor Prophet book with more messianic prophecy than any other. Among those prophecies is this one: "Shout and cheer, Daughter Zion … Your king is coming! He will be a good and righteous king, a humble king riding a mere colt of a donkey. God says there will be no more war, no more chariots or war horses in Jerusalem, no more swords and spears or bows and arrows. This king will offer peace to the nations, a peaceful, worldwide rule."

March, A.D. 33

On Sunday the crowd that had arrived for the Feast of Unleavened Bread heard that Jesus was entering Jerusalem. Some that had been with Jesus when He raised Lazarus from the dead were spreading the story and the crowd grew and grew. They welcomed Jesus as He rode into the city on a young donkey just as Zechariah predicted. People broke off palm branches and went out to meet Him, cheering, "Hosanna! Blessed is He who comes in God's name! He is the King of Israel!"

The Pharisees were frustrated. "That's it," they said. "The whole world is following Him!"

Some God-fearing non-Jews were in town to worship at the feast. Coming to Philip, they asked, "Sir, we want to see Jesus. Can you help us?" Philip told Andrew and together, they told Jesus. Jesus answered, "It's time for the Son of Man to be glorified." The Jews were rejecting Him and the nations were showing interest.

Later He continued, "Judgment time is here. The ruler of this world will be thrown out, and when I am lifted up from the earth (on a cross) people from all nations will gather around Me."

Some in the crowd answered, "We understand God's Law to indicate that the Messiah lasts forever. How can it be that the Son of Man will 'be lifted up' as you say? Who is this 'Son of Man'?"

Jesus declared, "The light will be among you a little longer. Walk by the light so darkness won't destroy you. Walk in darkness and you get lost quickly. Believe in the light while you can and you will be children of light." Jesus said all this and then withdrew from them for a while.

Even though His birth was accompanied by many convincing proofs, they didn't believe.

Even though John had declared Him to be the Son of God, they didn't believe.

Even though He proved who He was with signs and miracles, they still didn't believe in Him.

He had come to His own people but they didn't want Him. That's why, in essence, Jesus said on that day, "That's it. It's time …" Now He was headed to the cross.

Still later that day Jesus pleaded with the crowd, "Whoever believes in Me, believes not just in Me but in the One who sent Me. Whoever looks at Me is looking, in fact, at the One who sent Me. I am Light that has come into the world so that all who believe in Me won't have to stay any longer in the dark."

Those who did want Him—those who believed in Jesus' name—He gave them the right to be God's true children.

On Sunday of His final week of ministry on earth, Jesus rode into Jerusalem as a triumphant king surrounded by an enthusiastic crowd, but then announced His impending death.

A Prophetic Discourse on the Mount of Olives

Since 19 B.C., King Herod, only half-Jew, had been courting the approval of the Jewish leaders by building a magnificent Temple. Although the main structure was completed in 10 years, work on it continued until A.D. 64 and thus was still under construction during Jesus' ministry.

On Tuesday, with His followers nearby, Jesus informed the Jewish leaders and a crowd that had gathered in the unfinished Temple that He would soon be leaving with this agonizing statement: "Jerusalem! Jerusalem! Murderer of prophets! You killed the ones who brought you God's good news! How often I longed to gather your children as a hen gathers her chicks under her wings, but you wouldn't let Me. And now you're desolate. But know for sure: you won't see Me again until you can say, 'He, the One blessed by God, is coming to reign.'"

That afternoon, with the sun beginning to set behind this amazing structure, Jesus' followers pointed out the massive building stones, each one a meter wide by five meters long.

Jesus responded, "You noticed those, did you? Listen. Not one of these will be left upon another. They will all be torn down."

Jesus and His followers left the Temple and sat down on the Mount of Olives, looking back over at the Temple and the city. His disciples approached and asked Him, "When will that happen? (When will the Temple be destroyed like that?) How will we know when You will return? What signs will indicate this age is ending?"

When Jesus' followers asked these three questions, they probably thought one answer would deal with all three questions and that the questions were synonymous. Even though Jesus' answer was extensive and seemed to run together, he described three distinct events. At one point in His answer, He described the time in A.D. 70 when Titus would sack Jerusalem, destroy the Temple, and Gentile dominance of Israel would begin. Looking back on it now, it is easy to see that part of His discourse answered the question, "When will that happen? (When will the Temple be destroyed like that?)"

Jesus also told His followers that many would come saying, 'I am the Christ,' but not to be deceived. He said that there would be many wars and talking about wars, but the end still was not near; this will just be the beginning of birth pains. Then He gave a description of what Jesus called the Great Tribulation that is still future. This seems to be Jesus' answer to the question: "What signs will indicate this age is ending?" The "end of the age" they are speaking of is the end of Gentile dominance. The Great Tribulation marks the beginning of the end of that age. He then says, "But be ready to run when you see the abomination of desolation that Daniel spoke of set up in the Holy Place." That is the marker for the second half of the Tribulation. This will be a horrific time of judgment on Gentiles and Israel alike.

Finally, He clearly answers the question, "How will we know when You will return?" He says, "Right after the Tribulation, the sun, moon, and stars will be affected, heavenly powers will be shaken. Then the sign of the Son of Man will fill the skies—no one will be able to miss it. People who are unprepared all over the world will lament as they watch the Son of Man come from Heaven in a blaze of glory. With a blast on the trumpet He will dispatch His angels to bring home God's chosen ones all over the earth."

Two days following His triumphal entry into Jerusalem, Jesus gave a prophetic discourse to His disciples in which He told of future events that would shock the world.

Jesus' Last Supper with His Disciples

The day the Passover lamb was to be sacrificed, Jesus knew the time of His death was near. He wanted to warn His followers one last time and encourage them about the future, so He had Peter and John prepare the meal in a special place. He then reclined with His followers at the table and said, "You can't imagine how I have anticipated eating this meal with you before I suffer. I'll not eat it again until we share it together in the Kingdom."

He took the cup at the beginning of the meal, blessed it, passed it around, and said, "I'll not drink wine again until God's kingdom arrives." He also blessed the bread, broke it, and gave it to them with a metaphor, saying, "This is My body, given for you. Break and eat it like this as a reminder of what I have done and will do for you."

At the end of the meal He lifted the final ceremonial wine cup and initiated another symbolic remembrance: "This cup is the New Covenant, My blood poured out for you for the forgiveness of sins."

Jesus' followers' minds were swimming. So much was changing. As Jesus mentioned the New Covenant, their minds must have gone back 600 years to Ezekiel and Jeremiah's first mention of the New Covenant: complete forgiveness and cleansing; Yahweh would be their God and they His people; He would give them a new heart and write the Law on their hearts. This would be established through the shedding of Jesus' blood? That's what He said. Wait, shed blood? Jesus was going to die? Their concern must have shown on their faces.

Jesus continued. "Don't worry. You trust God, right? Trust Me, too. There is plenty of room for you as well in My Father's home. I'm leaving to prepare the way; to get things ready. Then I'll return and get you so we can live there together. You know the way I have to take."

Thomas wasn't so sure. "Master, we don't know where you're going. You expect us to know the way?"

Jesus said, "I am the Way. I am the Truth. I am the Life. No one can know God the Father or arrive in His house apart from Me. To know Me is to know the Father. Seeing Me is seeing Him!"

Then Philip spoke up. "Master, show us the Father and we will be happy."

"Philip, after all this time with Me, you still don't get it? You see Me, you see the Father. So why say 'Show us the Father'? Don't you believe that I am in the Father and the Father is in Me? What I am saying are not empty words I speak on My own. The Father, residing in Me, is working through Me. Either believe Me when I tell you that I am in My Father and My Father is in Me or believe because of the works you see Me do."

If Jesus' followers were struggling before, imagine now. Jesus couldn't have said it any plainer: He is God. They had been eating with God at the table! They had traveled and spoken and lived with God in the flesh for three years. And yet, He was leaving. He was going to die. Why? How?

Jesus comforted them again. "I will talk to the Father. He will provide you another Friend, a Counselor, so you will always have someone with you: the Spirit of Truth. Ungodly people won't receive Him—they don't have a clue. But you know Him already. He has been staying with you, and will even be in you!"

Here was more information for His followers to ponder. They had read Ezekiel's prophecy telling how the LORD God would put His Spirit in them as part of the New Covenant. Now Jesus— God, according to what He had just said—spoke of the Spirit of Truth that would be in them.

Jesus continued. "I want you to know before I go: the Counselor Friend, the Holy Spirit whom the Father will send in My name, will make everything plain to you and remind you of all the things I have told you. Rest in the unparalleled peace I leave with you and know that you are not being abandoned. Don't be upset. Don't be afraid."

The last supper that Jesus shared with His disciples was a Passover meal, at which time He explained the significance of His death and instructed them about His future care for them.

Betrayal of Jesus

We live in a world of people, creatures, and things we can see, touch, and hear. We call it the visible or natural world. But God, who is invisible, influences our world. In fact, God's angels and Satan and his demons are also invisible and influence our world often in ways we usually don't see or perceive. Jesus was aware of the invisible, supernatural world. He knew His time to die was approaching; Satan was working hard to make it happen.

As the Passover drew near once again, the leading priests were trying to figure out how to kill Jesus without upsetting the crowd. Satan entered into Judas (one of Jesus' 12 closest followers) and influenced him to contact the priests and betray Jesus to them when no one was around. They were happy to pay Judas for this, so he left looking for such an opportunity.

On the night of the Passover meal, Jesus wrapped Himself in a towel and performed the most meaningful act of love and condescension in Jewish culture; He washed His followers' feet—including Judas'—and explained the significance of that act. As He finished, He said, "If you understand what I do you will happily do it, too. But, of course, not all of you will." Then Jesus quoted part of Psalm 41, saying, "He who ate my bread has lifted his heel against me." As Jesus continued, He was more and more troubled. Finally He stated clearly, "It's true, one of you will betray Me." Later He even said, "The betrayer is the one to whom I give this morsel of bread I have dipped," and He gave it to Judas.

At that point, Satan entered into Judas again, and Jesus told him to "do it quickly." Judas was the treasurer of the group, so everyone thought Jesus was referring to paying for the meal or giving money to the poor. As soon as Judas received the bread, he went out into the night.

Later Jesus led His followers across the Kidron Valley to Olive Press Garden[21] on the Mount of Olives where He told them, "Pray that you won't succumb to temptation." Then He Himself went a little farther to pray. Jesus prayed earnestly, "Father, deliver Me from this impending suffering and separation from You, but only if it accomplishes Your will." Three times He prayed these words in agony, His perspiration falling to the ground like huge drops of blood.

Judas knew where they would be. He led armed soldiers, officers, leading priests, and Pharisees to the garden with torches and lanterns. Jesus, fully aware of what was to befall Him, stepped forward and asked, "Who are you looking for?" They answered, "Jesus of Nazareth."

Jesus, with all the power of the Old Testament name for God behind Him, answered, "I am," and they fell backward to the ground! He asked them again, "Who are you looking for?" and again, they said, "Jesus of Nazareth." Jesus answered, "I told you that I am. If I am the one you want, let these men go."

Peter had brought a sword. He drew it wildly now and cut off the right ear of Malchus, the high priest's servant. Jesus healed the man's ear and said to Peter, "Put your sword away. I accept the suffering the Father has planned for Me. Don't you realize that I could call to My Father and He would immediately send Me more than 70,000 angels?"

Turning to the mob led by the priests, He said, "You come after me with swords and clubs as if I were a robber? I was in the Temple day after day and you never touched Me. This is the time you chose, night; and this is the power you chose, the power of darkness."

Other times Jesus simply disappeared from their midst when they tried to kill Him. Now was the time. He willingly submitted Himself to the soldiers because He willingly submitted Himself to God's will.

---

21 Gethsemane means "olive press."

When one of Jesus' 12 disciples (Judas Iscariot) betrayed Him, Jesus did not resist arrest but willingly submitted Himself to the Jewish religious leaders and Gentile Roman soldiers who seized Him.

Jesus' Appearances before Unjust Judges

It was a terrible, mixed-up night. The perfect, pure, innocent Son of God appeared before sinful men in trial after trial. After the mob of soldiers and religious leaders arrested Jesus and bound Him, they took Him to Annas, the great patriarch of the high priestly family. He and his five sons had been the high priest and now his son-in-law had that position, but Annas was the de facto authority. He questioned Jesus and sent Him to his son-in-law, Caiaphas, the acting high priest.

The whole Sanhedrin was there trying to get people to lie about Jesus so they could kill Him, but they could not agree. Finally, they got two people to say the same thing. Caiaphas said to Jesus, "In God's name, tell us if You are the Christ, the Son of God."

Jesus answered simply, "You said it." But then He added, "Listen, from now on you will see the Son of Man coming on the clouds seated at God's right hand." Jesus was claiming to be the Son of Man (the Messiah) described in Daniel 7, at which they were outraged!

Caiaphas tore his clothes, yelling, "He speaks blasphemy! Why do we need any other witnesses? You all heard His blasphemy!" Then he called for a vote. While they spit on Him, struck, and slapped Him, the vote came in: "He deserves death."

But they couldn't kill Jesus legally, so the entire group brought Him to the governor of the Roman province of Judea, Pontius Pilate. There, needing a civil or political accusation for which Rome might put someone to death, they accused Him of misleading the nation, forbidding the Jews to give tribute to Caesar, and claiming that He was king instead of Caesar. Pilate asked Jesus, "Are You king of the Jews?" Like before, Jesus answered, "You said it."

But Pilate told them, "I find no guilt in this man." Frantically, they replied, "He stirs up the people with His teaching all over Judea, from Galilee to here." When Pilate learned that Jesus was from Galilee (Herod's jurisdiction) he sent Him off to be judged by Herod, who was visiting Jerusalem at the time.

Now since Herod had wanted to see Jesus for a long time, he was delighted that Pilate sent Him over. He was hoping Jesus would do something spectacular. He fired question after question at Jesus, but He didn't answer even a word. All the while the Jewish leaders multiplied their words with harsh accusations. Herod was offended at Jesus' lack of answers so he mocked Him. His soldiers joined in and contemptuously dressed Jesus in elaborate, kingly clothing and sent Him back to Pilate for Jesus' fifth trial that night.

Pilate called Jesus' accusers before him and said, "You claimed this man disturbed the peace. In your presence I examined Him and found your charge untrue, as did Herod, who sent Him back to me. It is clear to me that He is innocent, and certainly does not deserve to die. I'll just warn Him with a good whipping and let Him go."

The accusers went crazy: "Get rid of Him! Give us Barabbas!" (who had been imprisoned for rioting and murder). Pilate didn't understand and tried to release Jesus again.

"Crucify! Crucify Him!" the mob shouted back at Pilate.

"But for what crime? He doesn't deserve to die. I'm warning Him and letting Him go." Pilate tried to free Him for the third time. But the mob, not to be quieted, kept demanding crucifixion and finally wore Pilate down. He saw he was getting nowhere and that a riot was imminent, so he gave them what they wanted: a murdering insurrectionist on the loose and an innocent man at their disposal. (Pilate pardoned Barabbas and had Jesus whipped and handed over for crucifixion.) Then he symbolically washed his hands in view of the crowd, saying, "The responsibility of this man's death is not on me; it's totally on you."

The crowd responded, "We take the blame for His blood, as will our children."

Although Jesus was never proven guilty of any wrongdoing in any religious or civil court, He was unjustly flogged and condemned to die by Roman crucifixion.

The Crucifixion of Jesus, His Humiliation & Suffering

After the mockery of a trial, Pilate's soldiers took Jesus into the governor's palace and called their entire company together. Stripping Jesus of His clothing, they dressed Him in bright red. They devised a crown from thorns and put it on His head. They put a hollow stick in His hand to serve as a scepter. Then bowing in mock reverence, they addressed Him, "Honor to you, King of the Jews!" Then they spit on Him and hit Him on the head with the "scepter." When it was no longer fun, they removed the red toga, replacing it with His own clothes, and took Him out to be crucified.

As was the custom for the condemned person, Jesus began to carry the heavy crossbeam to the crucifixion site. Along the way they came across a Cyrenian named Simon and made him carry the cross. When they arrived at "Skull Hill," they offered Jesus a mixture of wine and perfume as a painkiller. At first taste, Jesus refused it.

The soldiers nailed Jesus to the cross along with two criminals, one on His right, the other on His left. While waiting for them to die, the soldiers passed the time gambling for Jesus' clothes.

They wrote the "criminal charge" against Him and posted it on the cross above His head: This is Jesus, the King of the Jews. People passing by shook their heads and made fun: "Oh, You can tear down the Temple and rebuild it in three days? Let's see some of that power! Son of God, are You? Then come on down from the cross!"

The leading priests and religious scholars participated in the mockery: "He saved others, but He can't save Himself! The King of Israel could get Himself off the cross. We would believe in Him if He did that! He trusted in God. Let's see if God will rescue Him now; if He even wants Him! After all, He claimed He was God's Son, didn't He?"

Passersby, religious leaders, soldiers all derided Him. If that wasn't enough, the two criminals being crucified with Him joined in, too.

Mocked.
Rejected.
Numbered with criminals.
Forsaken, despised, naked.
Scourged.
Disfigured.
Heads shaken.
Passersby appalled.
Pierced hands and feet.
Considered stricken by God.
"He trusts God, let Him deliver!"

These are descriptions of Jesus at His death, right? Well yes, but these are prophecies David and Isaiah wrote in Psalm 22 and Isaiah 52 and 53 about the Messiah that was to come. Jesus fulfilled them in His excruciating, humiliating death that day on the cross.

Jesus was taken to a place outside of Jerusalem called Golgotha, where He was nailed to a cross and suffered great physical pain and humiliation.

ישוע הנצרי מלך היהודים
ΙΗΣΟΥΣ ΝΑΖΑΡΑΙΟΣ Ο
ΒΑΣΙΛΕΥΣ ΤΩΝ ΙΟΥΔΑΙΩΝ
IESVS NAZARÆNVS REX IVDÆOR

Jesus' Death & Its Provision for Mankind

A Bright Moment … before the Darkness

The day innocent Jesus was crucified between two deserving criminals, one of them mocked Him. "You aren't much of a Messiah! Come down from there! Save us, too!"

The other criminal scolded his colleague. "You still don't fear God, do you? We're hanging here—both of us—receiving punishment we deserve. This man is suffering the same as we are, without having done any wrong." Then he pleaded, "Jesus, remember me when You enter Your kingdom."

Jesus replied, "Oh, I will. Today you join Me in paradise."

How could this be? A sinful, evil man utters a simple expression of faith as he is dying for his just punishment and he gets to go to paradise? New Testament writers, looking back on this event, wrote, "God proved His love for us, sinful, useless people, by sacrificing His Son … God put all of our wrongdoings on Him—the One who never did anything wrong—so we could have a right relationship with God … He carried our sins to death on that cross, taking sin out of the way so we could live proper lives. He healed us with His wounds. He brought us to God by making sure the payment for sin was cared for; the innocent paying the guilty ones' punishment."

At noon, darkness settled over everything until about 3:00 p.m. The sun appeared to burn out. Jesus' voice could be heard groaning deeply and crying out loudly, "Eli, Eli, lama sabachthani?" ("My God, My God, why have You forsaken Me?")

All this happened on a hill outside the city. In town, many people still went about their normal day. People did their regular feast day preparations and activities. Priests were at work in the Temple.

A thick curtain hung in the Temple prohibiting entrance into the Holy of Holies. The curtain was God's way of protecting men from certain death—the sentence for sinful man entering the presence of Holy God. At this point, that thick, tall curtain tore from top to bottom—ripped into two pieces! The earth seemed to tremble under an oppressive, invisible weight; rocks split in two. Tombs opened up and many believers, dead and buried, rose from the dead.[22]

Then, Jesus called loudly, "Father, I give You my life!" and breathed no more.

The captain of the guard—everyone there—observed the earthquake and all the events surrounding Jesus' death. They were amazed. The captain exclaimed, "This must be the Son of God!"

Joseph from the town of Arimathea was a good man with a servant's heart who lived expectantly, watching for God's kingdom. Although he was a member of the Sanhedrin, he had not agreed with the Council in killing Jesus. Joseph went to Pilate and asked for Jesus' body. He took Jesus' body down from the cross, wrapped it in a linen shroud, and buried it in a brand-new tomb carved out of solid rock.

The Sabbath (resting day) was about to begin, so some women who were companions of Jesus noted where the body was placed and went home to prepare spices and perfumes for Jesus' burial. Then during the Sabbath they faithfully rested and waited. They waited until Sunday to treat the body for its final burial.

---

22 After Jesus' resurrection, these people left the tomb area, entered Jerusalem, and were seen by many others.

Just before Jesus died on the cross, one guilty man who was being crucified beside Him placed his faith in Jesus and was granted the gift of life in a paradise beyond the grave.

NEW
TESTAMENT

ANTICIPATION
ARRIVAL
SECLUSION
POPULARITY
OPPOSITION
SUFFERING
VICTORY
APOSTLES
CHURCH
TRIBULATION
KINGDOM
JUDGMENT
RESTORATION

The Resurrection of Jesus Christ

Early Sunday morning, Mary Magdalene, Joanna (James' mother), and some other women brought the spices they had prepared to the tomb. Since the huge stone covering the entrance was rolled out of the way, they walked right in. But when they didn't find their Master's body inside, they were confused.

All of a sudden, two men in unusually bright clothing appeared. The awestruck women prostrated themselves before them.

"Why look for the Living One in a tomb? You won't find Him here. He is alive, raised from the dead! Don't you remember? He told you back in Galilee that He had to be killed on a cross by evil men and in three days rise." So they left and told the Eleven and everyone else the news. The women kept trying to convince the apostles, but they didn't believe a word. They thought the women were delusional! Finally, Peter jumped up and ran to the tomb. He crouched down and looked in. He saw grave clothes, nothing else. He left perplexed, not sure of what had happened.

Mary went back to the tomb, too. Confused, eyes filled with tears, she had an encounter with someone she thought to be the gardener, but when the man said, "Mary," she knew it was Jesus. "Teacher!" she cried.

"Now don't cling to Me. Soon I will be ascending to the Father. Go tell My brothers this: 'I am going up to My Father who is your Father, My God who is your God.'"

So Mary told the disciples, "I saw the Master!" and told them everything He said to her.

That same day two of the disciples were walking the seven-mile trip to Emmaus village. As they walked, they were deep in conversation about all the recent tragic events. Jesus came up in the middle of their conversation and walked beside them, but He kept them from recognizing Him.

"What are you talking about so intently as you walk?"

They stopped and just stood there, looking like they had lost their best friend. Then one of the two, Cleopas, said, "Are You the only one who hasn't heard what's been going on around here lately?"

"What has happened?"

"Jesus the Nazarene was a prophet from God. He did and said amazing things because God blessed Him. All the people loved Him! But our high priests and leaders betrayed Him, sentenced Him to death, and crucified Him. We had hoped He was the Messiah and would deliver Israel. This is the third day since they killed Him and now we are really confused! Some of our women went to the tomb this morning and couldn't find His body. They returned with a story about angels who said Jesus was alive. Others went to verify their story and found the tomb empty as the women said, but—no Jesus."

Jesus responded: "Can't you see? Can't you understand? Can't you believe the prophets? Didn't the Messiah have to suffer and be glorified?" Then He explained everything the Scriptures taught about His life and ministry, starting with Moses' books (at the beginning!) and going through the Prophets' books (the end of God's revealed word at that time).

Arriving at the entrance to Emmaus, Jesus acted as if He were going on to the next town. The friends objected.

"Stay, eat with us. It's late; daylight is gone." So He went in and sat down at the table with them. He took the bread, blessed, broke, and gave it to them. That's when they recognized Him! But as soon as they saw Him, they saw Him no more—He disappeared.

Then the two of them couldn't stop talking … "Wasn't that amazing?" "My heart was burning when He revealed the meaning of the Scriptures." "Mine, too …" as they hurried back to Jerusalem to tell the others.

On the third day after Jesus died and was buried, God raised Him physically from the dead to demonstrate God's power over sin, death, and Hell.

Appearances & Impact of the Resurrected Jesus

Late in the evening on the day Jesus rose from the dead, Cleopas and his wife[23] rushed back to Jerusalem and burst into the room where Jesus' followers were gathered. They heard the others speaking. "It's true! The Master has been raised up—Simon saw him!"

Cleopas said, "We saw Him, too!" and recounted what had happened on the road and how they recognized Jesus when He broke the bread.

As they spoke, Jesus Himself suddenly stood in their midst and said, "Peace be with you."

Since they thought they were seeing a ghost, they were frightened. Jesus comforted them. "Why the fear? Why the doubts? See My hands? See My feet? It's really Me! Go ahead, touch Me; prove I'm not a ghost. Ghosts aren't made of flesh and bone like I am."

Filled with joy and amazement, they stood there in disbelief. It all seemed too good to be true. So Jesus asked for food. They gave Him a piece of leftover fish, and He ate it right before their eyes.

That night Thomas, one of Jesus' closest followers called "The Twin," was not with them. So some of those who had been there told him, "We saw the Master."

But he replied, "I don't believe it. I need to see the nail wounds in His hands, put my finger in them, and stick my hand in His side or I won't believe it."

The next week His followers were in the room again, but this time Thomas was with them. Even though the doors were locked, all of a sudden Jesus stood in their midst and said, "Peace to you."

Turning to Thomas, He said, "Put your finger in the wounds in My hands; verify that they are real. Put your hand in the spear wound in My side. Don't continue in your faithlessness. Believe."

Thomas responded, "My Master, my God!"

By now many of Jesus' followers had clearly seen Him more than once. They touched Him. They saw Him eat. He stood among them. They heard His voice. They observed His mannerisms and saw His wounds. They could say without a doubt that Jesus had risen bodily from the dead.

Twenty-five years later, Paul of Tarsus cited several sightings of the resurrected Jesus (including one time when 500 believers saw Him at once) as an integral part of God's good news: Jesus died for our sins, was buried, and rose on the third day all in accordance with the Writings of God's prophets. He went on to say that he (Paul) saw Him as well. For them, there is no question: Jesus died but is now alive.

When Thomas exclaimed, "My Master, my God!" almost two thousand years ago, he was declaring his transformation from skepticism to a belief not only in Jesus' resurrection, but in His deity. Jesus responded with a benediction for future hearers of this good news: "You believe because you saw Me with your eyes, Thomas. Blessed are those who believe without seeing Me."

John, one of Jesus' closest followers, wrote a book about Him so that his readers would "believe that Jesus is the Messiah, the Son of God, and that by believing, may have life in His name." Thomas and the others saw, touched, heard, and believed. Those who did not have that privilege down through the centuries have based their belief on the New Testament writers' proclamations, Old Testament prophecies fulfilled, Jesus' claims and miracles, and the fact that Jesus' body was never found.

---

23 Some believe that the disciples Jesus met on the road to Emmaus were Cleopas and his wife.

After Jesus' resurrection, His disciples grew in their understanding that God had raised Him bodily from the grave and that He truly was the Son of God, the promised Savior.

Great Commission

On the evening of the Sunday Jesus rose from the dead, His followers were meeting behind locked doors for fear of the Jewish leaders. All of a sudden, without coming through the door, Jesus was standing there with them. First, He calmed these fearful friends. "Peace to you." Then He shared His plan with them for spreading the good news.

"Just as the Father sent Me, I am sending you. I want you to go into the entire world and share the good news with everyone. Remember how I told you before that everything written about Me in the Law and the Prophets and the Psalms must be fulfilled? That's what you need to share with people around the world."

Then Jesus explained what that meant so that when He was done, His followers understood the following:

· He was the Satan Conqueror promised to Adam and Eve in the garden.
· God would bless all families, peoples, and nations (the promise to Abraham would come through Him).
· That blessing—a right relationship with God—was made possible through Jesus' death on the cross and His resurrection.
· The Passover lamb was symbolic for Him, the Lamb of God who takes away the sin of the world.
· All of the Feasts and the sacrificial system gained their meaning in His perfect sacrifice for sin on the cross.
· He was pierced, beaten, whipped, unjustly condemned, had our sins laid upon Him, all according to God's good plan to crush Him, cause Him grief, and make His life an offering for sin.

· God's plan for Israel to declare His glory among all nations and peoples would finally take place through Him.
· God's name would be honored by people of other nations from morning till night.

Summing up, Jesus stated clearly, simply, the message His followers were to declare to all people groups: "You see now, it was written long ago that the Messiah would suffer and die and then rise from the dead on the third day and that this message—'Sins are forgiven for all who repent and trust in His name'—would be proclaimed to all the nations, beginning in Jerusalem."

His 11 closest followers went to a mountain Jesus had indicated in Galilee. He met them there and said, "With all God-given authority I commission you: As you go about serving Me, whether near or far, develop Jesus-followers from all people groups, teaching them to follow and practice my teachings, and identifying them with Me through baptism in the name of the Father, Son, and Holy Spirit. You can do this because I will be with you every hour of every day until this age comes to an end."

Jesus may have reiterated these marching orders other times to His followers. We don't know. But 40 days later, just outside Jerusalem, He told them one last time, "The Holy Spirit will come on you and enable you to tell others about Me here in Jerusalem and all over Judea, up into Samaria, and even to the end of the world."

When Jesus met with His disciples after His resurrection, He commanded them to go into all the world and make disciples from all the nations of the world.

Ascension of Jesus

After His death, Jesus presented Himself alive to His followers several times in different settings over a period of 40 days, providing indisputable evidence of His resurrection. At times He spoke one-on-one with friends. At times He ate meals with them and talked about the kingdom of God. As they met and ate meals together, He told them to stay in Jerusalem and wait for the Father's promise.

"I told you about this promise before. John baptized with water; very soon you will be baptized by the Holy Spirit."

The last time they were together, Jesus' followers asked Him, "Master, now are You going to restore Israel's kingdom? Is this the time?"

"That's not something you need to know. The timing is all up to the Father. But you will receive something special: the power of the Holy Spirit. When He comes upon you, you will have the ability to be witnesses of what I did and will continue to do. You will be My message carriers not only to people in Jerusalem, but all over Judea, next door in Samaria, around the world, and back again!"

Jesus was finished talking. He began to rise. His followers looked on, amazed! He continued to rise and before long, clouds covered Him. His followers just stared up at the clouds, dumbfounded. Would He appear again? Would He come back down? They weren't sure what to think.

Jesus passed into and through the clouds right up into Heaven. Although Jesus' followers on the Mount of Olives were confused, He must have been greeted with shouts and songs of praise as He returned to Heaven. Then a hush probably came over them as God's voice was heard.

"Sit at My right hand, the honored, most privileged place, until I make Your enemies a stool for Your feet. Just as I declared—and My Word stands forever—You are the permanent mediator; like Melchizedek of old, only better."

On that day Jesus began a new ministry as High Priest. Knowing what it was like to be a man with weaknesses and testing, having experienced it all—all but the sin—Jesus could be the one and only mediator between God and man. He was perfect man and holy God. That's why we can come to Him courageously to receive His mercy and grace. Jesus became our guarantor of a right relationship between us and God! His blood opened a new and living way for us by tearing down the barrier that existed. He now mediates that new covenant.

Back on earth, Jesus' followers looked back and forth across the sky, eyes searching the clouds for another glimpse of Jesus, their feet glued in place. They didn't want to leave. Suddenly, out of nowhere, two men in white stood beside them and addressed them. "O Galileans, why are you gazing at clouds? Jesus has gone to Heaven—you saw it happen! But one day He will return just like you saw Him go." So His followers left the Mount of Olives and walked the half mile back to Jerusalem.

After 40 days of preparing His disciples for their future roles, Jesus repeated His Great Commission to them and then ascended to Heaven to begin His ministry as our heavenly High Priest.

The Gospel & Jews in Jerusalem

Fifty days after Jesus' death and resurrection, Jerusalem was bustling again with Jews speaking different languages. Pentecost had come and with it faithful Jews from all over the Mediterranean world representing at least 14 different countries.

Jesus' followers were all together in one place. Suddenly, just as Jesus promised, the Holy Spirit came upon each of them with a sound like a gale force wind filling the building and what looked like tongues of fire over their heads. The Spirit enabled them to speak different languages.

The devout Jews that were celebrating the feast heard the sound and came running. Arriving at the house, they each heard their language being spoken and were thunderstruck.

Heads spinning, confused and bewildered, they spoke with each other: "Aren't these all Galileans? How can we be hearing them talk in our mother tongues? They're speaking our languages, describing God's mighty works! What's going on here?"

Some didn't seem to understand any of what was spoken (possibly those from Jerusalem who spoke only Greek or Aramaic), so they joked, "They are drunk on cheap wine."

Then the Eleven stood up in front of the crowd. Peter stepped forward and, using a passage from the prophet Joel, boldly explained they were not drunk, but that the Spirit of God was working in ways they had not seen before, but would be common in the future. He went on.

"Listen carefully, Israel. The miracles and signs God did through Jesus the Nazarene are common knowledge, evidence of God's working through Him. But according to God's precise plan He was betrayed by men who had their own ideas about law. They handed Him over to you, and you killed Him, nailing Him to a cross. But God freed Him from death's grip; death couldn't hang on. David described this centuries ago:

God is always with me, He's always at my side,
So nothing, no one moves me, I'm happy to abide.
In Him I have my hope, He'll lead me all the way,
Through Hades low. Corruption? No!
His Holy One won't stay!
Delivered at my death, I know the path to life;
Your presence brings me joy, and freedom from all strife.

"Friends, we all know full well that our ancestor David is dead and buried; we've seen his tomb. But as a prophet, knowing that God had promised a descendant for His throne, he looked ahead and wrote of the Messiah's resurrection ('He'll lead me all the way, Through Hades low. Corruption? No!') God raised Jesus up—we're all witnesses! Now, from the right hand of God, He poured out the Spirit, which is what you are seeing and hearing. David didn't ascend to Heaven, but prophesying, he said, 'God said to my Master, "Sit at my right hand until I make your enemies a stool for resting your feet."'

"Know this without a doubt: God made Jesus Whom you killed on a cross the Master and Messiah."

The Holy Spirit used Peter's message to cut through the façade of many. They knew he was right so they asked, "Brothers, what should we do now?"

Peter answered, "It's time for a change. Turn from your old ways to God. Then be baptized in the name of Jesus Christ, demonstrating your genuine faith in Him. Your sins will be forgiven and you'll receive the gift of the Holy Spirit."

How exciting it must have been for Peter and the others when about 3,000 believed and were baptized that day!

Soon after Jesus ascended to Heaven, His disciples began to proclaim the good news about who Jesus was, what He did, and why people should trust in Him as their Savior.

Life & Ministry in the Early Church

On the Day of Pentecost, the church was born in Jerusalem and began to grow phenomenally. Many of the people making up the church were from as far away as Mesopotamia and Libya—and everywhere in between. They had come to celebrate the Feast of Pentecost and saw and heard the coming of the Holy Spirit in power on the original followers of Jesus. They heard Peter's sermon, repented of their sins, and trusted Jesus personally. They experienced such a change that many of them did not return home immediately, but remained in Jerusalem.

Their new spiritual brothers and sisters who lived in Jerusalem and the surrounding areas made room for them in their homes. Some of these sold what they had to help the visitors. Others distributed goods and did what they could. Some have called it communal living, but what this new institution experienced was a voluntary, unselfish movement to care for the needs of the growing church, bulging not only with resident members, but with so many that were still away from home.

They met often—even daily—to hear teaching about the Savior from the apostles. They worshiped and prayed together and participated in the new ceremony they were calling "The Lord's Supper." They talked and worked and helped one another side by side (fellowship). These actions so characterized the fledgling church that people could see the Christ-followers were truly devoted to the church and its functions. Their lives were changed and others noticed. As people saw the change, their awe and curiosity drew them to Christ Jesus and His church.

But changed lives weren't the only attraction for curious onlookers. The church's leaders were performing what could only be classified as miracles, signs, or wonders. But these signs would not continue past the first century. God was simply validating this message (salvation through Jesus' death and resurrection), just as He validated Moses' message and Israel's nationhood through the astounding miracles that were limited to those times.

And it worked. People were drawn to God's church through the authenticity of its new believers, convinced the message was from God through the signs performed by its leaders. With such a foundation, the church members met confidently for worship and went out boldly to tell others about God's goodness and grace.

One time, while Peter and John were teaching, the Jewish leaders, indignant that they were instructing the people and proclaiming Jesus' resurrection, had the temple police throw them in jail. Even still, many of those in the crowd had already believed and the church's number grew to about 5,000!

The next day, the rulers, religious leaders, and scholars met with Annas the Chief Priest, Caiaphas, John, and Alexander to interrogate Peter and John. The Holy Spirit filled Peter and he said, "Rulers, leaders, if you brought us to trial for helping a sick man, I want you to know—we have nothing to hide. By the name of Jesus of Nazareth, Messiah—the one you killed on a cross and God raised from the dead—by means of His name this man is standing strong and healthy. Salvation only comes through Him. No other name has been or will be given to us in the entire world by which we can be saved."

What a message! He didn't back down on Jesus' resurrection or the exclusivity of Jesus as the only way to God. He couldn't. Without the resurrection and Jesus' unique sacrifice there is no good news! Every day they were in the Temple and in homes, teaching and preaching Christ Jesus, not letting up for a minute. This city-shaking, world-changing church started as a tiny group of 120, grew to 3,000, then 5,000, and continued to multiply.

Those who trusted in and followed Jesus assembled regularly to worship God, pray, study His Word, and fellowship together, maintaining a zeal to proclaim the good news to others.

The Gospel to the Fringe of Judaism

As the church in Jerusalem grew rapidly, a wave of persecution erupted. Saul, the lead persecutor, was maniacal in his efforts, devastating the church. He burst into home after home, dragging believers off to jail. Forced to leave the church's birthplace, Jesus' followers (except for the apostles) scattered throughout Judea and Samaria. But wherever they ran, they proclaimed the message about Jesus.

Philip also proclaimed the Messiah's message in a Samaritan city. But before Philip arrived, a man named Simon posed as a famous magician, dazzling the Samaritans with wizardry. For quite some time young and old had been in awe of him, thinking he had supernatural powers, and called him "God's Power."

But Philip came to town and announced the news of God's kingdom, proclaiming the name of Jesus. When the people heard Philip's message and saw the miraculous signs of God's validation (lame healed, evil spirits cast out), they listened eagerly. Many believed in Jesus and were baptized. The city exploded with newfound joy! They forgot about Simon, who himself believed and was baptized. Simon clung to Philip, fascinated by the signs God performed through him.

The apostles, still in Jerusalem, received the report that Samaria had accepted God's message, so they sent Peter and John to pray for them to receive the Holy Spirit. They laid their hands on them, and they did receive the Holy Spirit. When Simon saw what he thought was a new and amazing trick, he tried to buy it. "I want to be able to do that, too. I'll pay you whatever it takes!"

Peter said, "Death to you and your money! You can't buy God's gift or participate in God's ministry by making deals or offering bribes. Your heart, full of bitter envy and captive to sin, is not right before God. Repent now and ask the Master to forgive you for trying to manipulate God to get rich."

Peter and John left, continuing to spread God's salvation message in every Samaritan town they passed through on their way back to Jerusalem. But an angel of God told Philip to head south to the desert road that goes from Jerusalem to Gaza, so he did. The Finance Minister for Queen Kandake of Ethiopia was coming down the road. The government official had been on a pilgrimage to Jerusalem and was returning home, reading the prophet Isaiah.

The Spirit led Philip to the official, so he ran up beside the chariot and heard him reading this passage from Isaiah: "As a sheep led to slaughter, and quiet as a lamb being sheared, he was silent, saying nothing. He was humiliated and deprived of justice. And what of his descendants, since his life was taken away?"

Philip broke the ice. "Do you understand what you're reading?"

"How can I without some help? Please sit with me; enlighten me. Here's my first question: Is the prophet talking about himself or someone else?" Philip took the opportunity to proclaim Jesus to the Ethiopian using the Isaiah passage as his principal text.

As they continued down the road, they came upon water. The official said, "Here's water. Is there any reason why I can't be baptized?" So they stopped, went down into the water, and Philip baptized him then and there. When they came up out of the water, the Spirit of God suddenly snatched Philip away! The official never saw him again, but he continued down the road, content and rejoicing.

Philip showed up in Azotus and continued north, preaching the message in villages along that route until he arrived at Caesarea. Through him the church got its start in getting the good news of Jesus to Samaria and to an African who had been a proselyte to Judaism.

Persecution against the Jerusalem church caused Philip to go to Samaria where he proclaimed the gospel, but then was led by the Lord to Gaza to lead an Ethiopian official to faith in Christ.

Conversion of Saul of Tarsus

Saul,[24] a Jewish leader, was very much opposed to Jesus Who had declared, "I am the way …" Because Saul believed followers of Jesus were being unfaithful to the one true God and their Jewish faith, he persecuted them. He led in the stoning of Stephen (one of the early servant-leaders of the Jerusalem church) and dragged other believers off to jail, uttering death threats with every breath. He received arrest warrants from the Chief Priest to arrest "Way followers" in Damascus, and bring them to Jerusalem.

When Saul was close to Damascus, he was suddenly dazed by a blinding flash of light and fell to the ground. He heard a voice: "Saul, Saul, why are you harassing Me?"

Saul responded, "Who are You, sir?"

"I am Jesus, the One you're hunting down. Now get up and go into the city where you'll be told your next step."

His companions were dumbstruck, hearing the sound but not seeing anyone. As Saul picked himself up off the ground he realized he was blind, so the others led him into Damascus. Three days passed with Saul in darkness. He neither ate nor drank.

Jesus spoke to one of His followers in Damascus named Ananias and told him to go to Straight Avenue and meet Saul who was there praying and would be expecting him. Ananias knew about Saul, that he had come to town with authority to take people to prison, but he obeyed. Jesus told Ananias, "I've picked Saul as My representative to take My Word to non-Jews, kings, and Jews; and in so doing he will suffer for my sake."

So Ananias found Saul, placed his hands on him, and said, "Brother Saul, the Master, Jesus Whom you saw on your way here, sent me so you could see again and be filled with the Holy Spirit." At that moment something like scales fell from Saul's eyes, and he regained his sight! Right then he got up and was baptized, identifying himself with Jesus. Afterward, he had a hearty meal to regain his strength after his three-day fast.

For the next several days Saul met Jesus' followers in Damascus and proclaimed in the meeting places that Jesus was the Son of God. They weren't sure they could trust him, saying, "Isn't this the man who wreaked havoc among believers in Jerusalem? Didn't he come here to arrest us and drag us before the High Priest in Jerusalem?"

That didn't bother Saul. He kept preaching and disarming the Jews in Damascus by proving Jesus was the Messiah.

Back in Jerusalem he tried to join the disciples, but they also were afraid of him, not believing he was a Jesus-follower. But Barnabas had faith in him and stood up for him before the church leaders. He told them about Saul's conversion on the Damascus Road and how in Damascus he had laid his life on the line by preaching boldly in Jesus' name.

From then on he was accepted and continued to preach his Master's name boldly even among the Jews outside of Jerusalem and Judea who were influenced by Greek culture. This one who first thought of Jesus as an impostor, lying cult leader, a false messiah, now proclaimed Him as the Messiah, the Son of God, the Lord and Savior of all who call on His name. Saul realized that he himself was a blaspheming, insolent rebel who needed Jesus' saving grace.

God radically changed the life of Saul of Tarsus, a man who zealously persecuted early Christ-followers, and then God commissioned him to become a prominent leader in the early church.

---

24 Saul (Hebrew) had a Greek name (Paul) as well. Later, he became better known by the name Paul.

NEW
TESTAMENT

ANTICIPATION
ARRIVAL
SECLUSION
POPULARITY
OPPOSITION
SUFFERING
VICTORY
APOSTLES
CHURCH
TRIBULATION
KINGDOM
JUDGMENT
RESTORATION

Conversion of Cornelius

Cornelius, a captain in the Italian Guard, was stationed in Caesarea. A good man who helped the needy and prayed regularly, he led his family and house workers to worship the living God. At about three o'clock one afternoon an angel of God appeared to him.

The seasoned soldier stared stupefied and finally asked, "Sir, why have you come?"

The angel said, "Send men to Joppa to get Simon Peter. He is staying at the tanner's house down by the sea."

Cornelius called two servants and a faithful attending soldier. He told them about the angel's visit and sent them off to Joppa.

The next day at noon as the three travelers were approaching town, Peter went up on the roof terrace to pray. Hungry and wanting to eat, Peter fell into a trance in which he saw something that looked like a large sheet held by ropes at its four corners descending to the ground. Every kind of animal, reptile, and bird you could think of was on it. He heard a voice: "Go ahead, Peter—kill, eat."

Peter said, "Oh, no, Lord. I've never had food that was not kosher."

Again, he heard the voice: "If God says it's okay, it's okay."

After it happened a third time, the sheet was pulled back up into the sky.

As Peter considered the meaning of the vision, the Spirit whispered to him, "Three men are at the door looking for you. Don't hesitate to go with them because I sent them." Peter went down and said to the men, "I'm the man you're looking for." He invited them in and made them feel at home.

The next morning he went with them, taking along some friends from Joppa. The next day Cornelius expected them and assembled relatives and friends. When Peter entered, Cornelius fell on his face in worship! Peter pulled him up. "On your feet! I'm human just like you."

Cornelius introduced Peter to everyone and Peter began: "You know Jews don't enter homes of other ethnicities. But God showed me that no people group is better than any other, so I came to share this exciting news: God plays no favorites! It makes no difference who you are or where you're from—if you come to God His way, the door is open. You heard about salvation through Jesus Christ in Israel, right? Well, God's making that salvation available to everyone.

"You heard about Jesus Who, anointed by the Holy Spirit and God's power, went throughout the country helping and healing those oppressed by the Devil. We observed everything He did in Judea and its capital, Jerusalem, where they crucified Him. But three days later God raised Him to life again! Not everyone saw Him then— He wasn't put on public display. God had handpicked witnesses beforehand—us! We had the privilege of eating and drinking with Him after He came back from the dead. God commissioned us to announce Jesus as His appointed judge of the living and dead and His means of forgiveness of sins for everyone who believes. The prophets also declare it so."

Even as Peter spoke, the Holy Spirit descended upon the listeners. Peter asked his friends, "Any objections to baptizing these new friends who have received the Holy Spirit exactly as we did?" No one objected, so they were baptized in the name of Jesus Christ.

What a day! Peter learned that anyone (even a Gentile) can come to God through faith in Jesus. Cornelius learned that everyone (even "good" people who fear God) needs to hear the good news of Jesus and believe.

In a vision God taught Peter that the way to peace with God through Jesus is open to all people, regardless of their ethnic and religious heritage, and then He demonstrated that truth by saving Cornelius, a Roman military officer.

The Church in Syrian Antioch

Because of the persecution against the church triggered by Stephen's death, Jesus-followers scattered all over Judea, Samaria, and beyond. Some traveled as far as Phoenicia, Cyprus, and Antioch (480 kilometers from Jerusalem!) telling their fellow Jews about Jesus as they went. Antioch was a major commercial hub for the Roman world with a population estimated as high as 500,000. Although the city had a large Jewish community (40,000), it had a rich blend of cultures, including Greek, Syrian, Phoenician, Arab, Persian, Indian, and Egyptian people. It's no wonder then that some of the scattered believers, citizens of Cyprus and North Africa, began sharing the message of Messiah Jesus with Greeks in Antioch. God blessed their efforts: quite a number of Greeks believed and turned to the Master.

When the Jerusalem church got wind of this, they sent Barnabas to Antioch to check it out. Now his real name was Joseph, but the church leaders called him Barnabas ("encouraging one") because he was always encouraging people. He had been part of the Jerusalem church from the very beginning and had sold his land and given the money to help other church members. When Barnabas arrived in Antioch, he saw that this was all part of God's plan; His grace was drawing people of different ethnicities to Himself. He encouraged them (There he goes again!), urging the believers to continue steadfast in their purpose of sharing Jesus with others. Barnabas himself worked with them, being enthusiastic and confident in the Holy Spirit, and the new church grew tremendously.

Barnabas must have enjoyed leading this new, flourishing church. But he knew he could use some help reaching people in this city rich in ethnic diversity. He had met Saul a few years back and remembered that he had disputed successfully with Greeks; God had used him to bring them to Jesus. He knew that Saul was from Tarsus, which wasn't that far from Antioch. So he went to Tarsus to find Saul and invite him to join them in the ministry at Antioch. The two of them ended up working together in Antioch for an entire year, meeting with the church and teaching many people. Changed lives attracted attention so people in Antioch began calling the followers Christians ("little Christs") for the very first time. What a validation of their ministry!

About this time some prophets came to Antioch from Jerusalem. One of them, Agabus, warned, by the Spirit's leading, that a severe famine was about to devastate the world. (The famine occurred during Claudius' reign.) So the Christians decided each would send whatever they could to help their fellow believers in Judea. Barnabas and Saul were sent to deliver the collection to the Jerusalem church. After they had delivered the relief offering, they returned to Antioch bringing John Mark with them.

By this time the church had grown strong and had a diverse, multiethnic leadership team: Barnabas, a native of Cyprus, a Jew from the tribe of Levi; Simeon, most likely from Africa, nicknamed Niger or "Blackie"; Lucius, a native of Cyrene in Northern Africa; Manaen, probably Galilean, brought up in the royal court with King Herod; Saul, native of Tarsus (a city in present-day Turkey), a Jew from the tribe of Benjamin, a highly educated Pharisee.

These men were worshiping the LORD God and fasting—seeking God's guidance—and then it came. The Holy Spirit directed them to commission Barnabas and Saul for a unique work. So, right then and there in the middle of their intense praying and fasting, their yearning to be obedient, they laid their hands on them. They commissioned them for missionary service and sent them off on their new assignment which had come directly from the Holy Spirit.

(To be continued …)

The gospel spread from Jerusalem to Antioch, a major cosmopolitan city in the Roman Empire, and a blended Jewish-Gentile church was founded that sent missionaries abroad.

Paul's First Missionary Journey

Sent out by the Holy Spirit and the Antioch church, Barnabas and Saul traveled 25 km to Seleucia and boarded a ship to Cyprus. They brought John Mark with them as an apprentice. The first thing the missionary team did when they landed at Salamis on the eastern coast of the island was preach God's Word in the Jewish meeting places. They continued this practice throughout the island until they reached Paphos where the governor invited them to preach God's Word in the court.

A counselor to the governor, a charlatan known as "Elymas the Magician," tried to distract the governor from believing. But Spirit-filled Saul confronted him: "You son of the devil, you faith-distractor, stop turning people from the Way to go down crooked paths. You're blinding them spiritually! Now you'll be blind." Instantly, he was immersed in a shadowy mist; he had to be led anywhere he went. When the governor saw this, he became a believer, amazed at the powerful teaching of the Lord.

Then Paul (Saul used his Greek name more and more now) and the team sailed on to Perga in Pamphylia. From Perga they traveled on to Antioch in Pisidia where they continued their practice of proclaiming Jesus in the Jewish meeting places on the Sabbath. Many non-Jewish God-seekers trusted in Jesus and the salvation message spread quickly. Some of the Jews thought their way of life was being destroyed and forced Paul and Barnabas to leave. Paul and Barnabas left a core of happy, Spirit-filled believers, and went on to the next town, Iconium.

In Iconium, the same story: They proclaimed their message in the Jewish meeting place, many Jews and non-Jews believed, Jewish nonbelievers sowed mistrust and suspicion in the minds of the people in the street, and the missionaries had to leave. Fortunately, they were able to stay a long time, sharing confidently with God corroborating their work with miracles and wonders. One day they learned about a plot to attack them, so they went on to Lystra, where they began preaching the good news again.

An ancient legend told of a visit by Zeus and Hermes to the area in which, disguised as men, they visited 1,000 homes. All denied them rest except for one poor couple who served the gods the best they had. The gods warned the couple of the flood they would send to destroy their neighbors. They fled to high ground where their home was transformed into a beautiful temple and they became priests of Zeus.

Paul and Barnabas, probably unaware of the ancient tradition, entered Lystra and saw a man, lame from birth, sitting in the street. As the man listened to Paul's message, Paul saw belief in his eyes. Paul shouted, "Up on your feet!" The man leapt to his feet and walked all around.

The crowd went crazy, shouting in Lyconian, "The gods have come down as men!" They called Barnabas "Zeus" and Paul "Hermes." The priest of Zeus brought a bull to sacrifice to them. Finally, Barnabas and Paul realized what was happening. They showed their sorrow by tearing their clothes. "What are you doing! We're not gods! We are simply men like you with a momentous message: abandon these empty superstitions and embrace the living God who made the sky, the earth, and everything you see. In the past God let all the nations go their own way, but He left His clues: the beautiful world He created, rain, healthy crops. With food to eat and beauty all around, mankind saw the evidence of a Higher Power."

Even with this intense pleading, Paul and Barnabas barely stopped the sacrifice. Then Jews from Antioch and Iconium caught up with them and convinced the crowd to stone Paul. They dragged Paul unconscious outside town and left him for dead. But as the disciples gathered around him, he gained strength and was revived. The next day he and Barnabas headed for Derbe.

Commissioned by the church in Syrian Antioch, Paul and Barnabas carried the gospel of Jesus Christ to Cyprus and regions of Galatia, now part of the country of Turkey.

The Jerusalem Council

Paul and Barnabas arrived back in Antioch at the church that had sent them out as missionaries. Soon afterward some Jews arrived from Judea insisting that Gentile believers must be circumcised to be truly saved. Paul and Barnabas protested fiercely. The church resolved the issue by sending Paul, Barnabas, and a few others to put it before the apostles and leaders in Jerusalem.

The Jerusalem church and its leaders received them well. Paul and Barnabas reported about how God had used them to reach non-Jews on their missionary trip. Some Pharisees who had become believers, but still held to their former religious traditions, dissented: "Pagan converts must be circumcised; they must keep the Law of Moses."

The church leadership called a special meeting to consider the matter. After an extensive debate, four people made concluding remarks. First, Peter reminded them how God had used him early on to reach pagans with the good news at Cornelius' house. Those people heard the good news, believed, and were cleansed by God's grace in exactly the same manner as Jews. Conclusion? People—Jews and Gentiles—become right with God by faith alone in Jesus and His work.

That quieted the room. Then Barnabas and Paul reported what God had done through their ministry among the other nations. Conclusion? God is continuing to bring non-Jews to Himself as they trust in Jesus alone.

James had the final word on the subject. "My dear brothers, Peter told us the story of God's grace to outsiders from the outset. This is in perfect agreement with the Scriptures. When Amos wrote of Messiah's coming to rebuild David's house, he said it would happen so 'all the nations who are called by my name may seek the Lord.'

"God declared He would do it and He is! He's always known He would draw the nations to Himself.

"So here is my decision: We shouldn't unnecessarily burden non-Jewish people who turn to God. Let's write a letter encouraging them to avoid offending Jewish believers who choose to continue to follow the eating practices they learned as children. While we're at it, we should probably encourage them to abandon the sexual immorality that characterized the pre-Christian lifestyles of many of them." Conclusion? God is saving non-Jews by His grace just as He said He would. Their lives should demonstrate what they received by faith alone.

Everyone agreed—leadership and church alike—to send a letter with Paul and Barnabas to Antioch. They chose two leaders in the church, Judas (nicknamed Barsabbas) and Silas, to accompany them.

They went to Antioch, gathered the church, and read the letter. How relieved and pleased the people were when they heard the church's decision! After the letter was read, Barsabbas and Silas, both good preachers, encouraged and strengthened their new friends there before they headed back to Jerusalem to report to those who had sent them. Paul and Barnabas stayed in Antioch, teaching and preaching the Word of God with the other teachers and preachers that had developed in Antioch.

In response to false teachers who came to Antioch, Paul and Barnabas traveled to Jerusalem to confirm the truth that Gentiles do not have to keep the Law of Moses to have their sins forgiven.

Paul's Second Missionary Journey

Paul's second missionary trip took him back to the churches he and Barnabas started on the first trip and then into southern Europe for the first time. In Philippi, a Roman colony and the main city in that region, Paul and his new colleague, Silas, went down to the river where they thought God-fearers would meet to pray. That's where God opened the heart of the first convert in Europe just as He had done in Palestine and Asia Minor. Lydia listened to Paul's message and trusted in Jesus, Messiah.

For several days, as they walked to the river prayer meetings, a slave girl psychic (she was possessed by a demon and made money for her owners by fortune-telling) drew attention to Paul's band by shouting, "These men serve the Most High God and show clearly the path to salvation!" The demon in her knew very well who the Most High God was and that Paul was spreading His fame. But whether Paul was concerned that the Philippians would have understood "Most High God" to mean "Zeus" or whether he thought the yelling and screaming detracted from the message, he finally had enough. That day, he stopped ignoring her ranting, turned around, and spoke to the demon: "Out! In the name of Jesus Christ, leave her now!" At that moment, the demon left.

Of course, the girl's owners were not happy with Paul. They threw him and Silas in prison on trumped-up charges of bankrupting them and disturbing the peace. But the Most High God Whom they served was not done with them. He sent an earthquake, opening the prison doors and loosening their chains! Even the jailer came to trust in Jesus Christ! After they were freed, they greeted the new believers, encouraged them to stay strong in their faith, and left for the next town: Thessalonica.

Paul and Silas (with their new helper, Timothy) started churches in Thessalonica and Berea, too. But in both towns, maddened mobs of jealous Jews attacked them. Paul escaped to Athens, asking Silas and Timothy to join him as soon as they could.

While Paul waited in Athens, the idols sickened him—the city was full of them! He reasoned in the Jewish meeting place with the Jews, but he also talked with people in the streets as they shopped. Some intellectuals (Epicureans[25] and Stoics[26]) heard him speak of Jesus and the resurrection, and perceiving that he was preaching something they had never heard of, brought him to the Areopagus[27] for a public presentation of his views.

So Paul stood and addressed the forum. "It is clear to me, Athenians, that you take your religion seriously. You have many shrines. I was fascinated by one inscribed 'to the god no one knows.' Let me introduce you to this god you worship in ignorance: The Master of Heaven and earth, the God Who made the world and everything in it, doesn't need our temples or us to run errands for Him; He can take care of Himself. He made us; we don't make Him. And He wants us to find Him, yet He's not remote; He's near. He gives us our very life. One of your poets rightly said: 'We are His children.' Since we are His children, how can we think we could chisel a god out of stone?

"The unknown is now known, so you need to respond. God expects a complete turnaround from people when they know about Him. He established a day when all will be judged by the One He has already appointed. The Judge's confirmation came when God raised Him from the dead."

When Paul said "raised Him from the dead," some laughed, but some wanted to hear more. Apparently, Paul didn't get to finish his speech that day, but some stayed and talked with Paul and believed in Jesus. Dionysius, a member of the Areopagus, and a woman named Damaris, were two of them.

---

25 Similar to modern deists, Epicureans believe in a supreme being(s) not involved in, indifferent to, and unable to change, human affairs.
26 Stoics are pantheists, believing that the universe (Nature) and everything in it (including mankind) is god.
27 Athenian political and judicial body, regulating public matters and providing forums for public lectures.

Paul chose new missionary companions and set out to revisit the churches established on the first missionary journey and after that extended his trip into Greece.

Paul's Third Missionary Journey

When Paul arrived in Ephesus,[28] a large, influential city in the Roman Empire, he went to the Jewish meeting place to persuade Jews about the true kingdom of God. After three months, resistance caused him to take the Jesus-followers to the Hall of Tyrannus, where he taught them daily. Over the course of two years both Jews and non-Jews from all of Asia Minor heard the message of the Master.

God did unusually powerful signs through Paul to counter the existing culture of magic in Ephesus. "Miracle workers" did tricks and illusions to glorify themselves. God used Paul to perform formerly unseen feats to turn people's attention to the all-powerful living God. People even took hand towels Paul used to mop sweat off his forehead while making tents and touched the sick with them. God would then heal their diseases and cast out demons from them. Now that's power! God, through Paul, through the cloth, to the infirmed!

Some traveling Jewish exorcists (con artists) tried what they considered Paul's "formula": "I command you by the Jesus preached by Paul!" One large family of a self-proclaimed high priest named Sceva tried this on a man, but the demon talked back: "I know Jesus, I've heard of Paul, but who are you?" Then the demon-possessed man attacked the seven exorcists, ripping off their clothes. Naked and bleeding, they fled as best they could. Everyone in Ephesus—both Jews and non-Jews—heard this story. The name of the Lord Jesus was feared and revered.

Many magicians and witches believed and abandoned their sorceries. They brought their incantation books and burned them publicly. The value of the books was estimated at 50,000 silver coins. A clash of religious worldview cultures had erupted and the power of God's Word was conquering Ephesus.

Demetrius, a silversmith who had become wealthy by manufacturing shrines to the goddess Artemis, employed several artisans. He gathered his workers and others similarly employed.

"Men," he said. "We were doing so well and now Paul has ruined our business by telling people that handmade gods are no good. People in Ephesus and all over Asia Minor are being persuaded.

"But it's not just our business that's going to the dogs. The temple[29]—one of the Seven Wonders of the World—of our famous goddess Artemis will end up a pile of rubble if she who is worshiped around the world is forgotten!"

The crowd exploded, running, yelling! "Great is Artemis of the Ephesians!" A confused, angry mob stampeded the stadium, dragging believers to the center.

The confusion was thick; some were yelling one thing, some another, most not knowing why they were there. Then the chant, "Great is Artemis of the Ephesians!" began and continued for more than two hours.

Eventually, the town clerk quieted the mob. "Ephesians, doesn't everyone know that our city is protector of glorious Artemis and her image that fell straight from heaven? So settle down! These men you've dragged in here have done nothing to harm either our temple or our goddess.

"Demetrius and his artisan guild can go to court or bring complaints to the regularly scheduled meeting. But there is no excuse for this unruly assembly. Rome does not appreciate rioting." Then he sent them home. Although the town clerk's worldview differed greatly from Paul's, he didn't want a riot.

Since Paul's missionary team faced opposition in Ephesus (as well as other places), he later wrote a letter to the Ephesians in which he warned, "Our strong God wants you to be strong in Him. Use the armor the Master has prepared for you so you can face whatever Satan puts in your path. We're not fighting against men, but against the Devil and his dark forces."

---

28 Two hundred thousand inhabitants, educational center with 25,000-seat amphitheater, center of magical arts and of popular Artemis cult.
29 Temple of Artemis, largest in Greek world, was 127 m x 67 m x 18 m high—four times larger than the Parthenon in Athens.

After a brief visit with the Syrian Antioch church, Paul made a third journey, spending time ministering in the very pagan city of Ephesus.

Paul before Roman Judges

Agrippa and Festus sat together in judgment of Paul. Festus was the newly appointed Roman governor over Palestine replacing the corrupt Felix. Agrippa, the part-Jew puppet king allowed by Rome to rule over Galilee and land east of the Jordan River, was eager to hear Paul's defense. He opened the trial: "Go on, tell us your story."

Paul took the stand and spoke. "My life from childhood is an open book. Just about every Jew in town knows my story and could tell you, if they are willing to admit it, that I lived as a faithful Pharisee, part of the strictest sect of Judaism. I am on trial today because of my wholehearted hope in the promise God made to my ancestors, who hoped for the same thing down through the centuries—the coming of Messiah. I believe He has come, was killed, and has risen from the dead. Is it so odd to believe that God can raise the dead?

"It's true. I, too, used to oppose this Jesus of Nazareth fervently as if in service to God. By authority of the high priests, I threw these believers in prison (not realizing they were God's people), and when called upon, voted for execution. I raided their meetings and tried to get them to curse Jesus. I even pursued them to foreign cities.

"While traveling to Damascus on one such mission, a flash of light brighter than the noonday sun above us shone on us. It was so bright, O king, that we fell to the ground. Then I heard a voice: 'Saul, Saul, why are you torturing Me? Why do you fight against Me?'

"I asked who this was. The voice said He was Jesus Whom I was persecuting! Then He told me He had a job for me.

"'I'm sending you to foreigners to open their eyes so they may turn from darkness to light, turn from Satan to God, that they may receive forgiveness of sins, and a place in My family by trusting in Me.'

"So, King Agrippa, I obeyed! I proclaimed the life-change Jesus desired (turning to God from the old way of life) right there in Damascus, then in Jerusalem and the surrounding countryside, and then to the whole world.

"It's for the 'whole world' part that the Jews grabbed me in the Temple that day and tried to kill me. But God has protected me. The Jews won't admit it, but Moses and the prophets wrote the same thing I proclaim: that the Messiah must die, be raised from the dead, and announce God's light both to Jews and to non-Jews."

Festus couldn't keep quiet any longer. He interrupted: "Paul, you're insane! Too much studying has driven you mad."

But Paul replied, "No sir, with all due respect, Festus, Your Honor, I am not mad. I speak the truth rationally. The king knows what I am talking about and has known for a long time. He doesn't miss much of what goes on here, and I'm convinced he didn't miss this—it was all done in the open. You believe the prophets, don't you, King Agrippa? I know you do!"

Agrippa answered: "For years I have watched this nation, but do you think you'll persuade me to become a Christian in such a short time?"

"That's my prayer. Whether quickly or not, I long to see you and everyone in this room become like me—trusting in Jesus that is, not in chains."

The king and his sister, the governor, and their advisors got up and went into the next room to confer. They agreed that Paul had done nothing to deserve prison, let alone death. Paul's story of his life before he responded in faith to Jesus, his life-changing encounter with Jesus, and his life after he trusted Jesus may not have convinced them to believe in Jesus that day, but it did convince them of his innocence.

At the end of his third missionary journey, Paul was arrested for his faith in Jesus and appeared before several Roman judges, where he boldly shared his personal faith story.

NEW
TESTAMENT

ANTICIPATION

ARRIVAL

SECLUSION

POPULARITY

OPPOSITION

SUFFERING

VICTORY

APOSTLES

CHURCH

TRIBULATION

KINGDOM

JUDGMENT

RESTORATION

Final Years of the First Century A.D.

If Paul had written a letter at the very end of his life which reflected happenings in the world around him and his final message to the church, it may have looked something like this:

I am nearing the end of my journey here on earth. Yes, I did finally get to Rcme and God allowed me to contribute significantly to the life of that growing, influential church, to Him be the glory!

However, as I write this letter, I am on my way in chains to Aquae Salviae (5 kilometers from the city) where Roman soldiers will separate my head from my body. I count it a privilege to suffer and die for my Savior as the prophets of old, James, Simon the Zealot, and now Peter have done before me. (My Roman citizenship guarantees me a more merciful death than that of our Lord and Peter and others.) With Nero's lunacy and the fact that it is now illegal to be a Christian, I fear all the apostles and many others will suffer a similar fate.

Since Nero burned Rome and blamed the Christians, informers are easy to find. And no longer is it necessary to prove accusations; it is open season on Christians. That's why many are in hiding. Only my dear friend Dr. Luke bravely accompanies me today.

Interestingly enough, as I go to my "judgment," we are not even sure why I will be put to death other than for being a follower of the Way. Some say it is Nero who insists on my death; others that the prefects of the city are behind my sentencing. No matter. God delivered me from the mouth of the lion and from shipwrecks, and from the Jews. Now I go willingly and without fear, counting it a privilege to live and die for the One to Whom I belong. I desire only that He be glorified whether in my life or my death.

Timothy brought Mark as I had asked in my last letter to him and was promptly imprisoned. I am thankful to God that he was released and now returns to his ministry. My major concern for him and others is not for their physical safety, but that they will stand firm and contend for the faith—that they will see the basic, essential teachings of Jesus and His sent ones as we see them.

> We look at Jesus and we see the invisible God!
> We look at creation and see Jesus' handiwork.
> We look at the Lamb and see the firstborn from the dead,
>   the Ruler of Heaven and earth.
> We look at the One who was judged and see Him
>   Who reconciles all to Himself through His death.

False teachers are turning believers away from the most holy faith. With Jude, I pray you all will build yourselves up in the faith. As I go to my death, I affirm that Jesus is the One we proclaim, warning all not to add to the message that is Jesus. No more, no less. Be mature in Him and battle for the faith.

During the final four decades of the first century, many Christians suffered persecution and martyrdom and false teachers began to corrupt the teachings of Jesus and His apostles.

Two Thousand Years of Church History

At any given time, a segment of God's Church has suffered persecution somewhere in the world while another has been blessed somewhere else in the world. That being understood, the story of God's Church from the early days after Jesus' return to Heaven and the death of His first followers, could be told in general terms in seven paragraphs describing seven periods of church history.

During the first 200 years (A.D. 100-300), the Church suffered **Persecution** throughout the Roman Empire. Men like Polycarp, a disciple of the Apostle John, were burned at the stake. Justin Martyr, while pursuing various schools of philosophy, was influenced by the fearless conduct of Christians such as Polycarp as they faced persecution. Martyr, too, was later tried (in 165) and beheaded for his faith.

Emperor Constantine embraced the Christian faith and established religious tolerance in the Roman Empire, bringing a period of **Popularity** (300-500). Augustine, considered the greatest influence in the ancient western Church, became a believer in Jesus Christ at age 32 partially through faithful prayers of his mother, Monica. The Church Councils of Nicea and Chalcedon, taking place during this period, declared that God's Son is true God (not created), and that Jesus was fully man and fully God, respectively.

A period of **Corruption** (500-1300) ensued as the Bishop of Rome emerged as a pope over the entire Catholic Church. Papal edicts and church traditions were elevated above the authority of the Bible, creating false doctrines and practices. Differences in doctrine and practice between Rome and Constantinople resulted in a schism between the East and the West. Interestingly enough, it was during this time of corruption that Muhammad of Mecca claimed he received a message from God, bringing the birth and rise of Islam. In response, many Western "Christians" led militant Crusades to free the Holy Land from Muslim Turks.

Wycliffe (b. 1328), one of the earliest opponents of papal authority, wanted all to have the Bible in their own language, so he translated the Latin Vulgate into English in 1382. His work and influence initiated a period of **Reform** (1300-1600) in which Martin Luther, the Anabaptists, and others challenged non-Biblical practices and returned to early church practices. Along with the influence of these brave men and women, the Gutenberg Press contributed greatly to the Reformation by making copies of the Bible available to everyone.

Skepticism followed. During this time (1600-1850), Immanuel Kant (German philosopher) and Friedrich Schleiermacher (known as the "Father of Modern Liberal Theology") encouraged movement away from seeing truth as revealed by God to the idea that truth comes through experience and reason.

An exciting return to **Outreach** (1725-1900) was led by the Moravians (started in Czechoslovakia by John Hus and later led by German Count Zinzendorf) who spread the gospel to many countries as early as the 1700s. Englishmen John Wesley and William Carey furthered the effort founding mission societies, while American D. L. Moody developed a practical ministry training school.

The Church has now moved into an era that could understandably be called **Divisions** (1850 to present). Cults, such as Mormonism, Christian Science, and Jehovah's Witnesses, have sprung up and spread around the world. Pentecostalism attempted to return to what they call apostolic faith by embracing the gifts of tongues and healings. Fundamentalism rose up in an effort to counter the effects of liberal theology in churches and seminaries. While these divided the Church, others now teach that all religions point to God (Religious Pluralism). Still, Christianity has spread around the world, but a Global Shift of its influence is moving from North and West to South and East.

For more than 1,900 years, since the death of John, the last living apostle, God has preserved His Church through much hardship and adversity and has caused it to spread all around the world.

Jesus' Return for Believers

The night before Jesus died, He told His followers He would be leaving, but would also come back, and take His followers with Him: "I know you are afraid, but don't misunderstand. You trust God. Now trust Me. There is plenty of room for you in my Father's home, you can be sure of that. But I'm going now—Myself—to get your rooms ready. Then I'll come back and get you so you can be with Me."

Over the next few days, Jesus died on a cross, was buried, and rose again. For 40 days after that, He talked, ate, and interacted with His followers until He ascended to Heaven.

So now we wait. Jesus' sent ones wrote about "waiting for our blessed hope," God's "Son from heaven," the "Savior, the Lord Jesus Christ."[30] But what does that mean, to wait?

I remember waiting with my sister for our father to come home from work. We would always wait for him to eat supper together. Sometimes I was lazy. I would wait sprawled out on the couch, watching television. But as soon as I heard my father coming up to the house, whistling as he came, I would jump up, turn off the TV, straighten what I could as quickly as I could and greet him cheerily as he walked in the door—not the best type of "waiting." However, when I was eager for his arrival because we had something planned, I would be up and about the house, preparing and eagerly, expectantly waiting. This is the kind of waiting Jesus desires of us.

But it's been 2,000 years since Jesus said He would return. Does He really expect us to be about His work, eagerly anticipating His return? Well, how many years passed from the time when Isaiah spoke of Immanuel coming to earth until Jesus was born? Or between the time David wrote Messianic Psalms until the Messiah came? How many years went by between God's promise to Abraham that all nations would be blessed by his descendant and the promise was fulfilled? Or from when God first promised a Satan Conqueror until Jesus went to the cross? One of Jesus' followers, Peter, clarified it a bit for us: "Don't forget, friends: for God, one day is as good as a thousand years, a thousand years as a day. God isn't 'taking His time' in fulfilling His promises—His timing is perfect."

But while we are waiting, some of our friends and family are dying. What about them? Jesus' followers asked that question. Paul, one of Jesus' messengers, remembered Jesus' thoughts the night before He died.

"Don't worry about those who have died while waiting; we don't grieve like those who don't have hope. In fact, they will be ahead of us. Since Jesus died and rose again, we believe that Jesus will bring with Him those who have already died believing. At the end of the age, Jesus will descend from Heaven with a thunderous command. As He comes down from Heaven, those believers who have died (but are currently fully alive and alert in God's presence in Heaven) will have their bodies raised first. Then we who are still living will be snatched from the earth to join them in the clouds where we will meet our Lord Jesus. What a wonderful day that will be! It won't be like walking on air—we *will* be walking on air. We can encourage one another with this message."

Adam's sin brought death. Jesus' life, death, and resurrection brought life. Because of Jesus, we won't all die. On that day when Jesus comes, the dead, rotting bodies of believers will become new, imperishable ones. In a flash our bodies will be transformed from fragile, corrupted bodies of sin to pure, immortal bodies.

Based upon the promise of Jesus and the teachings of the apostles, those of us who trust in Jesus expect Him to return at any time to take us to Heaven to live with Him.

---

30 Titus 2:11-14; 1 Thessalonians 1:9-10; Philippians 3:20-21.

Future Judgment of Believers' Works

From the Diary of an Imagined Athlete, A.D. 65

What a race! I can't believe I won. When I began training for the Isthmian Games of Corinth over a year ago I never thought I would win—it was an honor simply to be there and participate. As I trained, I was feeling strong; my times were good. But as we lined up for the start, so many good athletes side by side, we all knew only one would get the victor's garland. I did not expect to stand in front of all those people having the woven celery branches placed on my head.

Smiling, waving at the crowd, I couldn't help but think of what Paul wrote: "You've all seen the athletes race in the stadium. Many run; one wins. You need to 'run to win.' Those athletes train hard for a wreath that will wither and fade. You're after a crown that will last forever." I worked hard for those leaves adorning my head. I want to strive even harder to receive a crown from Jesus one day.

I know that I will stand before Jesus where He will sit in judgment of my works. He won't be determining whether or not I will spend eternity with God in paradise. His death on the cross and His resurrection took care of that. I simply needed to trust Him for my deliverance from sin. The judgment and reward I anticipate is more like what I experienced at the games. Paul wrote about it in a couple of letters he wrote to us (the Corinthians), but he also mentioned it in his letters to the Romans and to his pastor friend, Timothy.

I know that when I won the race today, I was rewarded for my faithfulness in working diligently to be the best I could at running. Jesus' judgment of my Christian works will be similar; He will judge what everyone can see: my works and my faithfulness in serving Him. But He will also judge what no one else can see: my inner motives and thoughts.

My prayer for today: "God help me keep my motives pure. I want to glorify You by receiving from Jesus, not a crown of leaves that die, but an imperishable crown at His judgment seat."

Sometime after Jesus returns for believers and before He returns as King, He will evaluate the lives of those who have trusted and served Him and will reward them for faithful service.

NEW
TESTAMENT

ANTICIPATION
ARRIVAL
SECLUSION
POPULARITY
OPPOSITION
SUFFERING
VICTORY
APOSTLES
CHURCH
TRIBULATION
KINGDOM
JUDGMENT
RESTORATION

A Future Period of Tribulation

From the beginning of time, God has progressively revealed Himself to us. We have come to know who He is, what He is like, and about His plan for us bit by bit as we read through His Word. He also informed us about the future in a progressive manner.

God began to tell His people about things still future to us (people of the twenty-first century) through Daniel and Ezekiel in the sixth century B.C. Centuries later, Jesus filled in some of the blanks with a message He gave on the Mount of Olives. Then John the Apostle pulled the puzzle together in his book of the Revelation. By looking at all of these writings, we can come to understand the principal question that the Jews had in Jesus' day: when would Messiah come? It was more complicated than they realized.

Daniel used "the decree to rebuild Jerusalem" as his starting point. Then he used difficult-to-understand formulas of sevens of years which included 7 sevens (49 years), 62 sevens (434 years) and one more seven (7 years)—70 sevens in all—to measure time until the Messiah would come. But Daniel also states that the coming Messiah will be cut off somewhere within those time periods (after the 62 sevens) and then the city and the Temple will be destroyed again by the people of a future evil ruler. He wrote that the end will come with its floods, desolations, and wars. And still there would be the final seven in which that evil ruler will make a covenant with Israel but will break that covenant halfway through its time, desecrating the Temple.

In 538 B.C. and 444 B.C. decrees went out and Jerusalem was rebuilt in 444. Jesus the Messiah came and was crucified hundreds of years later and within a short time afterward (A.D. 70), the Romans destroyed Jerusalem and its Temple. According to Daniel, these events would occur before the beginning of the seventieth seven. During that seven a ruler from the people who destroyed Jerusalem would come and desecrate the Temple by insisting he be worshiped in that place which was built for worship of the living God. For that to happen, an undetermined amount of time must pass before the 70th seven takes place—at least time for the Temple to be rebuilt! The period in which we are now living (called the Church Age by some) is that undetermined amount of time. The 70th seven will begin when a ruler who comes from the people that destroyed the city in A.D. 70 (Romans/Europeans) establishes a seven-year treaty with many Jews. Then halfway through the seven years, he will desecrate the Temple (presently still not rebuilt).

It is after those still future seven years of terrible suffering and tribulation that Messiah will come, destroy the beastly Antichrist ruler, and establish His kingdom.

God's judgment upon the Jewish people, which began in the time of Daniel and Ezekiel, will not be completed until a future period of seven years of tribulation.

The Return of Jesus Christ

God's prophets often spoke and wrote about "The Day of the Lord" referring to a lengthy period of time of God's judgment and establishment of His Kingdom on earth. We use "day" in a similar manner. My father would say, "In my day …" and launch into a nostalgic narrative about the good old days. When speaking about the late 1700s we might say, "In George Washington's day people didn't have refrigerators."

The Day of the Lord begins with the Great Tribulation and continues for many years after that (through something the Bible refers to as a 1,000-year reign of the Messiah). But after the Great Tribulation and before the millennial reign of Christ, something will happen that is described in the Bible as "on that day." That's when Jesus will come "with power and great glory." On that day someone might say[31] …

"Look, the heavens are opening! A rider called 'Faithful and True' is coming to earth on a white horse with His armies to judge and make war. No one can miss it—He and His armies are filling the sky! This is none other than the King of Kings and Lord of Lords, the Word of God who died and rose from the dead. His eyes are blazing! He sees right through to our hearts.

"But look, He is coming to protect the inhabitants of Jerusalem. He is opening a fountain to cleanse them from sin and cover them with grace. He is fighting their enemies—the godless nations who fought against Jerusalem—and His people will share in the spoils.

"High in the sky against the sun, a winged creature—I guess it's an angel—is calling out: 'Come to God's great supper! Feast on kings and leaders of all ranks and their steeds.' To whom is he calling? The birds?

"Now the Beast, that sinister world leader during the time of the Great Tribulation, has gathered his army from among all the kings and armies of the earth. They plan to fight against Jesus! But He speaks and the nations are struck down! The Beast and his False Prophet are captured and thrown into the Lake of Fire. All the rest are slain by the word of the One called 'Faithful and True.' Now come the birds. They are feasting freely on the flesh of the armies of the Beast.

"Oh, the earth is shaking—it's an earthquake! The mount to the east of Jerusalem is splitting in two! Half of the mountain is moving to the north and half to the south. Look! King Jesus is descending on His horse to what is left of the Mount of Olives. He's dismounting and standing before His conquered enemies. What shouts of victory from His hosts! What a day! The Son of Man has come in power and great glory!"

---

31 The narrative following is based upon Zechariah 12-14; Revelation 16 and 19; Matthew 24:29-31.

Shortly after His return for believers, Jesus will come back with those He took to Heaven and will deliver His redeemed people from their time of Great Tribulation.

The Future Earthly Kingdom of Jesus Christ

For centuries, God's prophets (including David, Daniel, Isaiah, Jeremiah, Micah, and Zechariah) spoke of the Millennium—a 1,000-year reign of the Messiah—as if they believed it would be a literal, lengthy kingdom on earth.

"God's kingdom will topple, crush, and finish off the other kingdoms for good." (Daniel)

"You are my Son. I will give you the nations for a present, the far reaches of the earth as a gift." (David)

"Every person on earth will see the glory of the Lord." (Isaiah)

"David's descendant will bring safety and security to Israel and Judah." (Jeremiah)

"Weapons of destruction will be made into farm tools; all will enjoy peace and prosperity." (Micah)

"The LORD will attack … on that day He will stand on the Mount of Olives east of Jerusalem." (Zechariah)

"Your son, Mary, will be great. God will give Him David's throne to rule Israel's kingdom forever." (Luke)

Even Jesus, when together with His followers for the last time, did not negate the future kingdom. They asked if He would restore the kingdom to Israel then or at another time. He replied, "The time is not for you to know, the timing is up to the Father."

According to Jesus' follower John, who knew his Master's kingdom was still to come, someone might describe its coming like this:

"An angel descended from Heaven, carrying the key to the bottomless pit and a massive chain. He seized the Dragon that old Snake—the very Devil, Satan himself—binding him in chains for 1,000 years. The angel locked him in the pit so he could not deceive the nations during those 1,000 years.

"Jesus took His throne and others took lesser thrones to rule with Him. Those who were martyred because they stood for Jesus and God's Word, refusing to worship the Beast, were brought to life and reigned with Jesus, also. Those who experience this, the first resurrection, are blessed indeed for the second death has no power over them. They are God's priests—Christ's priests—who reign with Him 1,000 years.

"But after the 1,000 years, Satan will be released for a short time …"

Following His return with power and glory, Jesus will fulfill the Old Testament promises to Israel of a Davidic king and worldwide kingdom by reigning over the earth for 1,000 years.

Satan's Final Doom

From pure and innocent to evil and deceiving.

From unparalleled beauty to appearance of beauty, but truly devilish hideousness.

From worshiping God and basking in His glory to suffering eternal torment in the Lake of Fire.

That's Satan, from beginning to end. God created him as one of the most beautiful, intelligent creatures of all. But he became proud; he wanted to be like God; he wanted to take God's place. So he was thrown out, cast down from his high position, taking other angels with him. At that point God prepared a place of eternal fire for him and his followers.

Then Satan began to tempt mankind. He started with Eve in the garden and won't quit until God judges him definitively. After Satan tempted Eve in the form of a serpent, God cursed him and declared war between Satan and the woman. He told Satan that a descendant from the woman would deal the crushing deathblow to him.

The Satan Conqueror came, born of a woman in Palestine at just the right time. His name was Jesus. He didn't fail when tempted by Satan. He completely and perfectly resisted temptations designed specifically for and aimed directly at Him. Many times during His life on earth Jesus demonstrated that He was more powerful than Satan and his demons by casting them out of people they possessed.

Then, on an historic day outside Jerusalem, Jesus dealt that crushing deathblow mentioned centuries earlier when He gave His life to free all mankind from Satan's power. That's why He came on the scene: to abolish and put an end to Satan's works. You see, since we are made of flesh and blood, it makes sense that Jesus took on flesh and blood, became a man. His death was the only way to rescue us. By embracing death He canceled out any hold Satan had on death and freed us who are afraid of and subject to death. Jesus' cross was the conquering blow against Satan, but it won't be fully applied until a future date.

During the Millennium, Satan will be bound. Imagine that, bound for 1,000 years and not able to influence mankind during that time. How wonderful that will be!

But at the end of that time, Satan will be loosed one last time. Think of it: he will certainly be frustrated and angry and ready to attack with 1,000 years' worth of schemes, machinations, and revenge. In a moment he will soar from his prison to launch his plan to deceive the nations—what he had done for centuries before. Satan will search high and low on earth for enemies of God. He will convince them to go to war against God, gathering the greatest human army ever, millions strong. They will advance on and lay siege to Jerusalem.

But as soon as they arrive, fire will course from Heaven and consume the armies. From among the smoldering, malodorous bodies, the one who deceived them will be whisked away and hurled into Fire and Brimstone Lake, where his servants, the Beast and False Prophet, will already be suffering. There they will continue in agonizing torment endlessly.

At the close of the earthly reign of Jesus Christ, after a brief final rebellion against God, Satan will be cast into the Lake of Fire where he will be punished with everlasting conscious torment.

The Great White Throne Judgment

One of Jesus' followers, John, lived a long time and told many people about Jesus in various places. When he was old (about 95 years old!), people that didn't believe his message put him in prison on an island called Patmos. While he was a prisoner, God gave John a peek into the future through a fascinating vision; it was as if he were taken to Heaven. He could see what was going to happen there and what was going to happen on earth—as if he were watching it happen right in front of his eyes! He wrote it all down in a book. Part of his vision included what would happen after Satan was thrown in Fire and Brimstone Lake. His book reads like this:

"I was in God's throne room and saw an immense white throne and the risen Jesus—to Whom God had given all authority to judge—seated on it. Earth and sky ran from His presence but could find no place to hide.

"Then I saw Sea coughing up all who had died there. Death and Hell turned their dead over, also. I saw all who had died, important people and people of lesser stature, stand before that throne! Books were opened, including the most important one: the Book of Life. The dead were judged by what they had done as recorded in the books.

"Then Death and Hell were thrown into Fire and Brimstone Lake which is the second death. Anyone whose name was not found written in the Book of Life (that book which contains the names of all those who received eternal life through the Lamb of God who takes away their sins) was thrown into that awful lake."

All those who refuse to know God (by not believing the good news of Jesus and trusting Him) will suffer for what they've done. Their sentence will be eternal separation from Jesus and His awesome power and love. If they refuse Him when they have the opportunity, they will be separated from Him forever.

Jesus Himself said, "This is important: anyone who believes me and believes the Father who actually put me in charge, has real, lasting life and will not be condemned These believers[32] have passed from the world of the dead to the world of the living."

---

32 Our final story tells about the future of these believers.

At the end of time as we now know it, unbelievers will stand before God to be sentenced to eternal punishment for their sins and their refusal to receive God's provision for sin.

The Destruction of the Heavens & Earth

A Conversation: Ben Believer and Scott Scoffer

Ben: God spoke and the universe came into being. In six short days God created stars and planets, water and land, plants and animals, man and woman. God then put mankind in charge of His creation, giving him much freedom and only one rule.

Scott: You really believe that?

Ben: Oh, yes. But man broke that rule and God cursed the ground and all creation. Creation had no choice in the matter, and now waits longingly to be freed from death and decay. Even God does not want to keep this creation going forever, but anticipates creating a new heaven and new earth.

Scott: Yeah, right. What about that? Jesus is supposed to be coming back, but the apostles and followers of Jesus down through the ages are dead and gone and everything is continuing like always since "God created it." Nothing changes!

Ben: In fact, things do change. God partially destroyed the world once already. Mankind became more and more evil, so God sent a flood to wipe evil off the face of the earth. Things got better, for a while. But man was at it again very soon afterward, sinning, corrupting. So the Eternal One who created this transitory world will one day be done mending. He will take the heavens and earth that are wearing out like old clothes, destroy them for good, and judge mankind in the process.

Scott: Yeah, yeah, if you believe that sort of thing.

Ben: Listen, God spoke and the world came into being. He spoke and the flood came. God will speak again to destroy those who don't believe, and the earth, planets, and galaxies will fuel the fire of judgment. In your skepticism you are overlooking something: a thousand years is like a day to God and a day like a thousand years.

Scott: Whatever. Maybe that's why God is being slow in coming through with His promise.

Ben: No! He's being patient for your sake. He doesn't want anyone to be destroyed. He wants us to repent. But that day will come when we least expect it, just like when a thief breaks into a home at night.

Scott: (mockingly) You think?

Ben: Without a doubt. And when it does, you like "Big Bang"? The sky will collapse with a thunderous explosion as Jesus releases the atoms (which He is now holding together as he supports everything in the universe by His powerful Word) to go their own way. Everyone's thoughts will be laid bare; all their works exposed and judged. What a terrible event!

Scott: (pensively) Whoa. So what do we do?

Ben: Unbelievers need to repent and trust Jesus as Savior. Believers should live godly lives in expectation of that day when God sets the heavens on fire and the elements will melt away in the flames.

At or near the time of the great white throne judgment of unbelievers, God will destroy the current sin-contaminated earth and its heavens with a roaring fire and intense heat.

NEW
TESTAMENT

ANTICIPATION

ARRIVAL

SECLUSION

POPULARITY

OPPOSITION

SUFFERING

VICTORY

APOSTLES

CHURCH

TRIBULATION

KINGDOM

JUDGMENT

RESTORATION

The New Heavens & New Earth

Down through the ages people have been waiting, longing to be free from the body captive to sin, and live forever with God. They have eagerly anticipated this ever since sin first entered the world.

It was literally paradise for Adam and Eve to live in the garden. But sin contaminated God's perfect world. Over the years God made it clearer and clearer to fallen humanity that He had a plan and would not give up on having righteous men and women live on a perfect earth. Many along the way came to understand this and submitted to God's plan.

Abraham was one of those. In all his sojourning he kept his eye on an unseen city designed and built by God Himself. Abraham's wife, Sarah, and then Isaac and Jacob had the same vision. All of them kept believing and didn't turn back when the road got difficult on their pursuit of a far better country than anything they had seen on earth—that Heaven country. God will honor them; He has a City waiting for them. Many more were pioneers, blazing the way, looking forward to the day God would reveal His City.

Where is this City? It's not on Mount Sinai; in fact, it's not even in Palestine. This is the City where the living God resides and judges. It's the City to which we have entrance only through Jesus' sacrifice. So where is it, or should we ask where will it be?

After Satan is thrown into Fire and Brimstone Lake, God's special City, the New Jerusalem, will descend brand-new, resplendent, and glorious from Heaven, prepared for God as a bride for her husband. A thunderous voice will come from the throne:

"Look! Look! God is moving in, making His home with men and women! He will wipe away the tears of His people. Death, tears and pain are finished, gone for good. All the old is gone."

Then the One seated on the throne will speak. "Listen! I'm making everything new. And this New City is what My Children, the faithful, will inherit. But degenerates, murderers, sorcerers, idolaters, liars—all the faithless—are destined for Lake Fire and Brimstone, second death!"

What is the City like? It will shimmer like a precious gem, filled and pulsating with light. The foundation will be garnished with every precious gem imaginable. The high, majestic walls of jasper will have 12 gates each made from a single pearl, an angel positioned at each. (By the way, the gates will never be shut.) The City will be laid out in perfect design—2,200 kilometers long, wide and high.

Main Street will be of pure gold, translucent as glass. There will be no Temple, for the Sovereign Lord God and the Lamb are its Temple. God's Glory serves as the sun for the City, the Lamb for its streetlights! There will never be night! All the nations will walk in its light. Earth's kings will bring the splendor, glory, and honor of the nations into the City.

At the center of the City is God's throne (and the Lamb's). God's glory will provide all the light anyone will ever need. Flowing crystal bright from the throne right down the middle of Main Street will be Water-of-Life River. The Tree of Life will be planted on each side of the river, producing twelve kinds of fruit, a ripe fruit each month. Its leaves will heal the nations.

Who will enter the City? Nothing dirty, detestable, or deceiving will get into the City. Only those whose names are written in the Lamb's Book of Life will get in. These servants of God will look on His face and worship, reflecting His character, and ruling with Him forever.

But God's story ends with wonderful news—everyone who has trusted Jesus as his or her Savior will enter a beautiful, sin-free paradise and live there eternally with God.

God's Story and You

So, what did you think of these stories about real people in real places in real time? Were you able to follow the one story woven through the many: the love story of Almighty God creating humans, loving them, and providing them with a way back to Himself?

We started with "No thing. No light, no color, no shape or sound" and ended with a city shimmering "like a precious gem, filled and pulsating with light, [its] foundation … garnished with every precious gem imaginable."

Early on in the story we saw a beautiful paradise created by Almighty God for His special creation: man and woman. But something went wrong. Humans chose poorly and became separated from the God Who loved them. Spiritual death (guilt, shame, fear, separation from the one holy God) was an immediate result. We saw humans choosing poorly time after time and rebelling against a holy God until we became convinced that rebellion and wrongdoing are a part of human nature. Sadly, we saw that death is the proper punishment for those evil actions called sin. Then, time after time, down through the ages we saw physical death as judgment for sin. At the end it became clear that there is another, final death that is eternal called the second death.

However, at the end of the story we saw beauty again—human beings living and worshiping the holy God in a glorious paradise. How did that happen? In the garden an innocent animal died in the place of the guilty. That pattern was repeated throughout history, creating hope and symbolizing the death of One Who would come, conquering Satan, sin, and death. Who would He be? Prophets gave predictions and psalmists made proclamations that seemed impossible. No one could fulfill these prophecies … unless he was God.

Then we saw a baby born one night in humble surroundings. In one evening many of the prophecies were fulfilled. The baby grew into a man who loved God and cared for people like no other ever had. More prophecies were fulfilled as He changed water into wine, healed people, stopped the wind and the waves, and cast out demons. He appeared to be God. Even in His death, this man fulfilled prophecies. Was this Jesus the Satan Conqueror?

Three days after dealing the deathblow to Satan's head, Jesus rose from the dead, proving He was a man like no other—He was God incarnate. He commissioned His followers to spread the good news about Him. The church was then born. Down through history Jesus' followers have passed this story along until it has spread around the world and arrived at this real time, this real place. You, a real person, have read that story.

Paradise will return. Relationship with God can be restored. The death of Jesus, innocent man and holy God, was the supreme sacrifice to provide forgiveness and bring us into a right relationship with God. Put your faith in Him. Trust Him and let His sacrifice be yours. Reserve your place in paradise.

The Roots of Faith Bible Resources

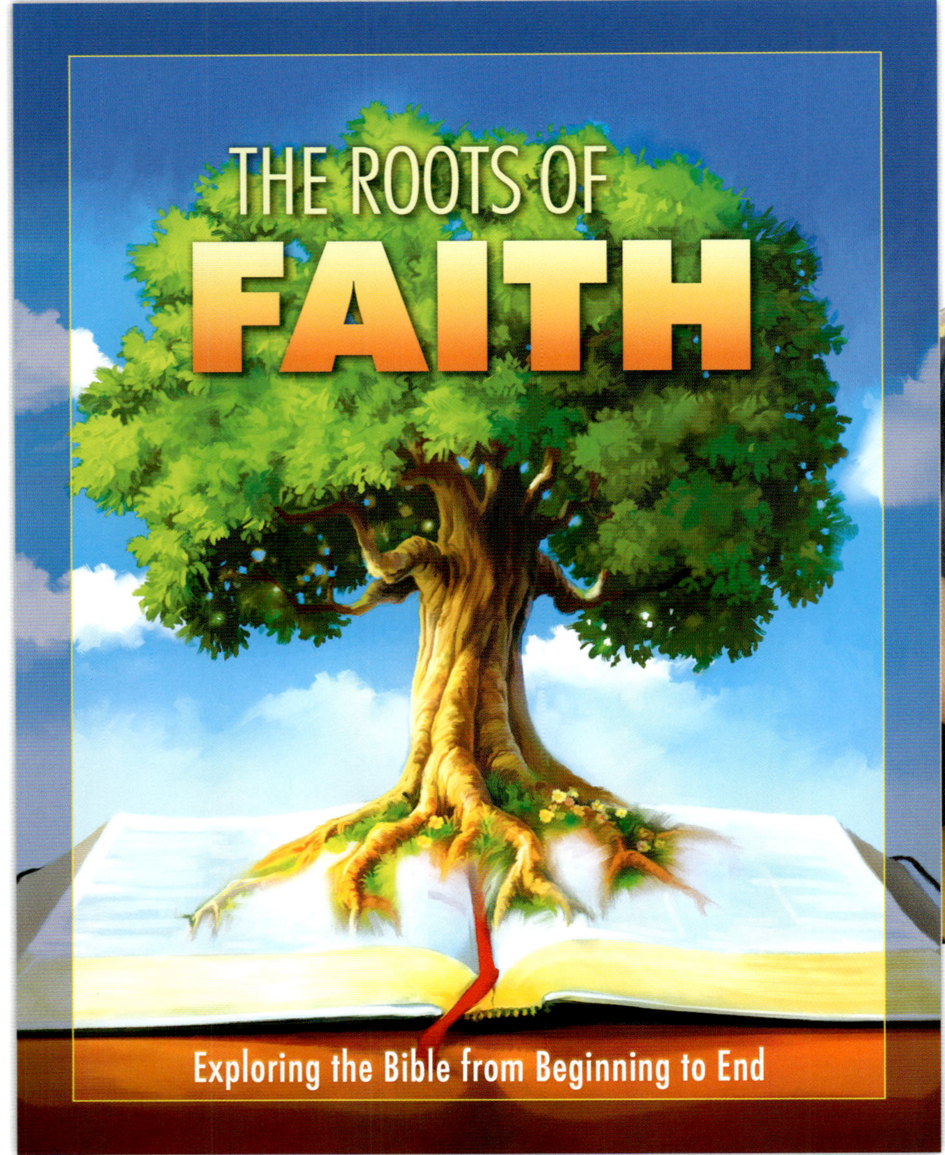

The Roots of Faith Old Testament and New Testament courses unfold God's redemptive story chronologically, from Genesis through Revelation, and focus on theological concepts that are essential for a clear understanding of the gospel of Jesus Christ. A complete Instructor's Guide is available for each course.

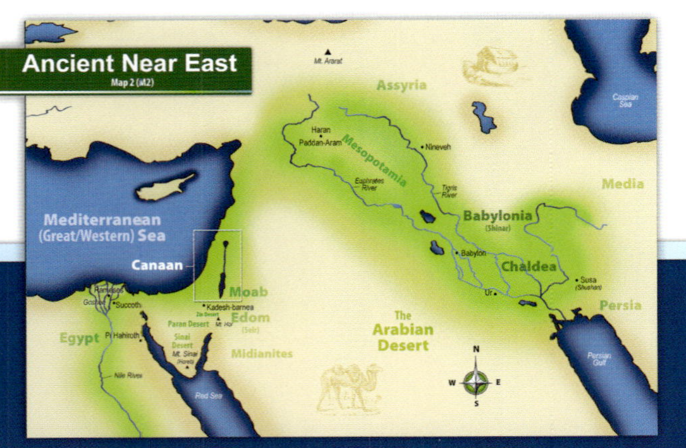

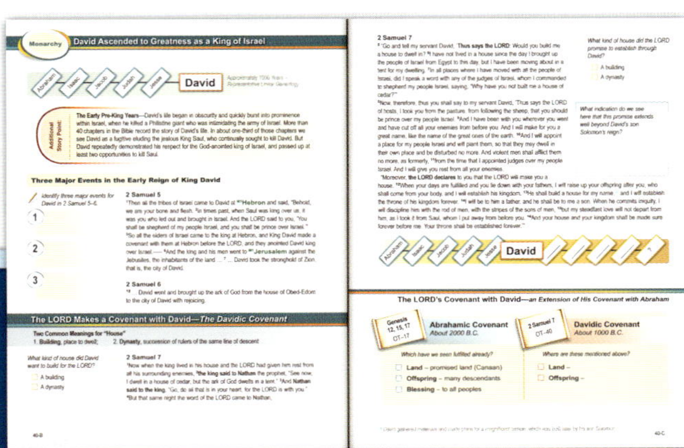

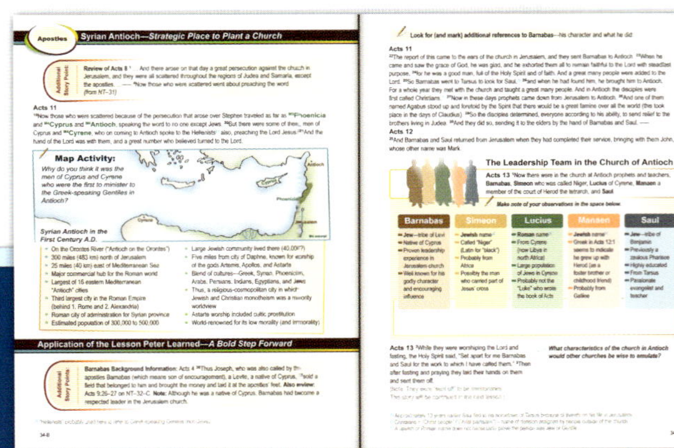

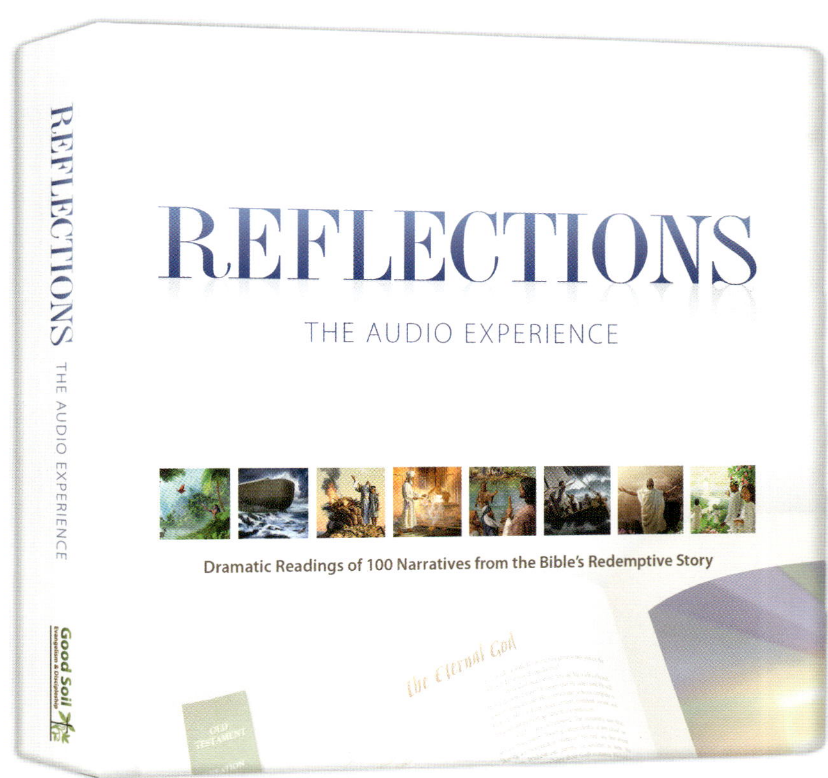

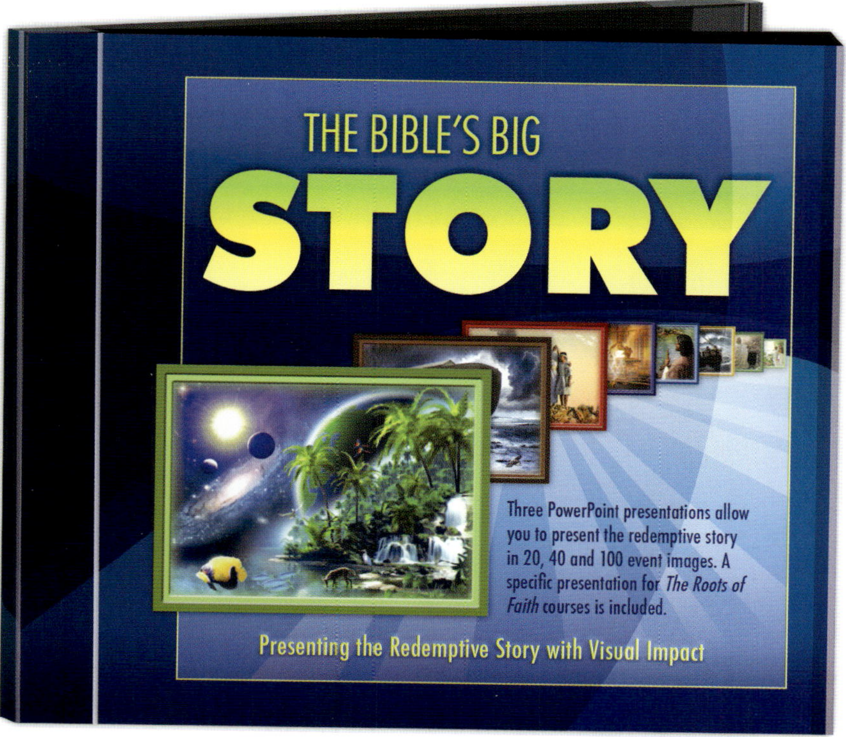

Reflections: The Audio Experience is a set of audio CDs containing dramatic readings of the 100 narratives contained in **Reflections from God's Story of Hope** and in **The Roots of Faith** course workbooks.

The Bible's Big Story CD contains three PowerPoint presentations for teaching the Bible's redemptive story. The presentations feature the Good Soil Redemptive Art Series images, but also include Old and New Testament Bible maps and the Chronological Bridge to Life.

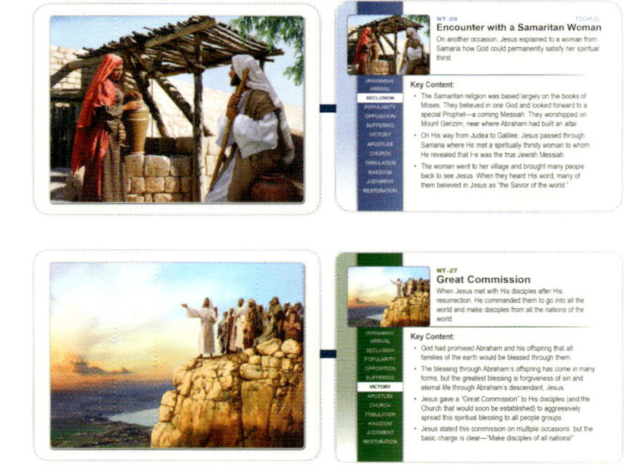

A set of **ChronoBible Cards** contains 135 pocket-size cards (4.5" x 3.375") for learning and reviewing the content and chronology of the Bible's big story. There is one card for each of 100 key Bible events and one card for each of the 25 major Bible eras. Also included is a bonus set of the 10 Chronological Bridge to Life cards.

Good Soil Evangelism & Discipleship

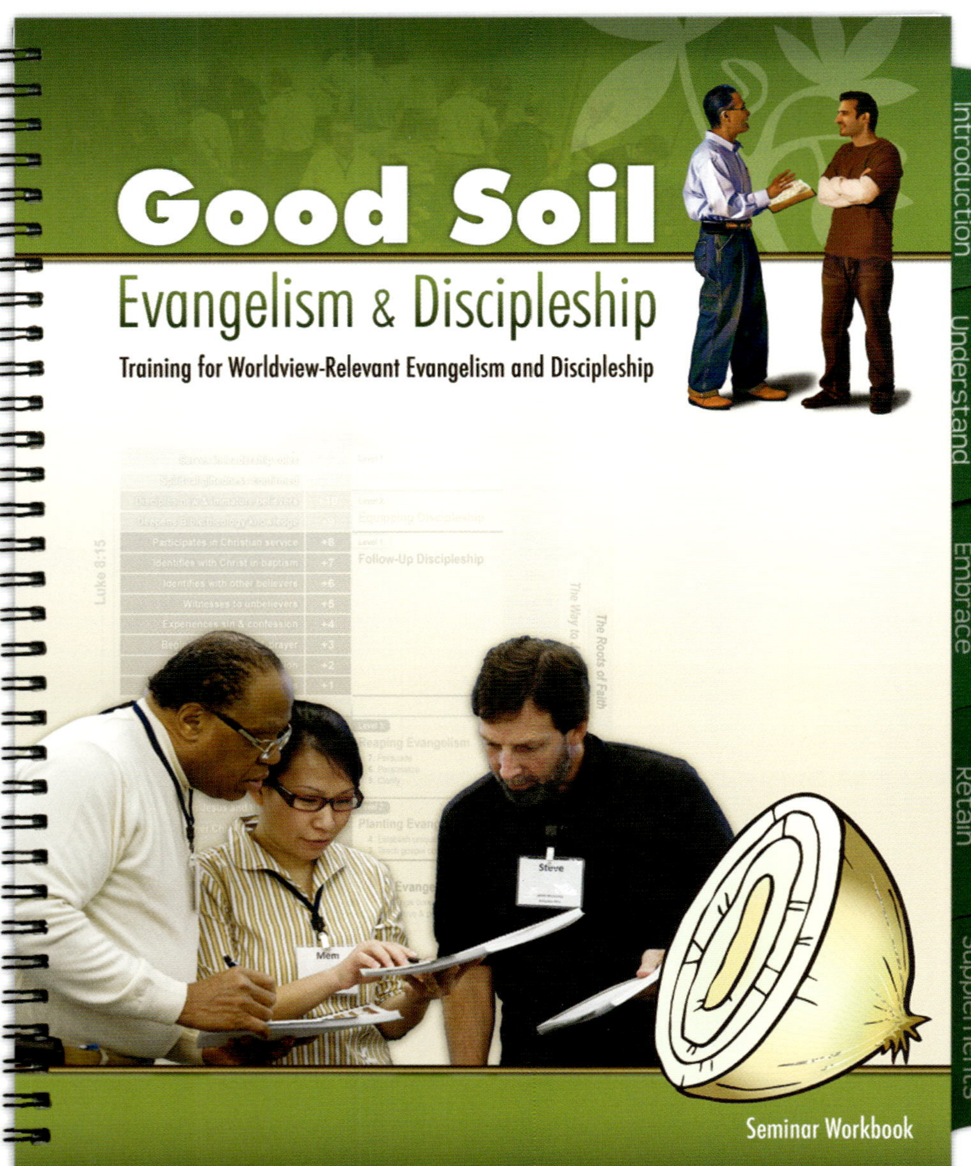

The **Good Soil Evangelism & Discipleship Seminar** offers two days of worldview relevant evangelism and discipleship training. Participants learn to share God's story of hope in a world of competing faiths and cultures in a way that people will clearly understand it, sincerely embrace it, and firmly hold on to it. An optional one-day **Trainer Certification Workshop** follows the Basic Good Soil Seminar.

Gaining Ground with Good Soil is a scaled-down version of the Good Soil Evangelism & Discipleship seminar embedded in an interesting missionary story format. Free (downloadable) study guides are available for personal study and for leading small group studies.

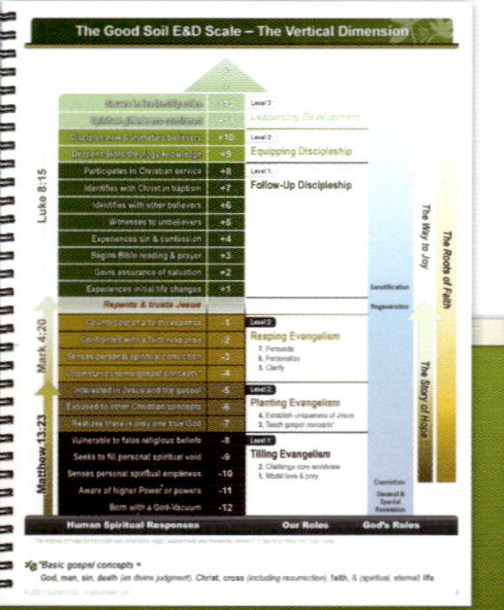

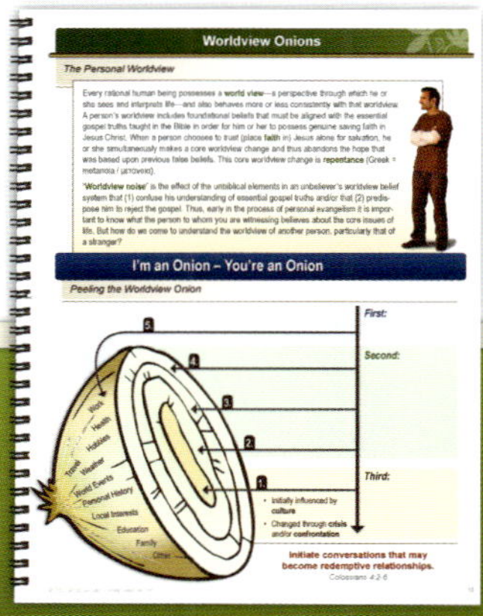

The Story of Hope is a time-flexible Bible study for presenting the Bible's redemptive story. Three formats are available: 40-page book, 60-page workbook, and a pocket-size booklet. Free (downloadable) Leader's Guides and ESL Guides are available. **The Story of Hope** has been translated into several languages.

The Way to Joy is a leader-guided basic discipleship study, intended primarily for use with new or spiritually undeveloped believers. Free (downloadable) Leader's Guide and Class Facilitator Guides are available. **The Way to Joy** has been translated into several languages.

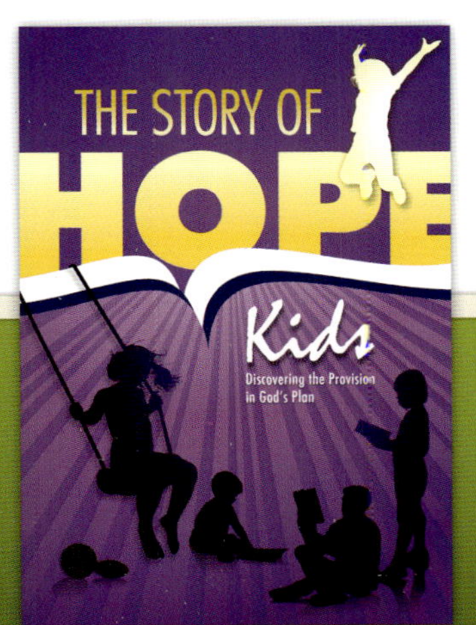

Kids Sing the Story of Hope
Sing-Along Music

The Story of Hope–Kids is a 60-page visual-design and language-level adapted version of **The Story of Hope** for kids ages 8-12. This workbook contains the same core content as the adult-level version. A free (downloadable) Leader's Guide is available.

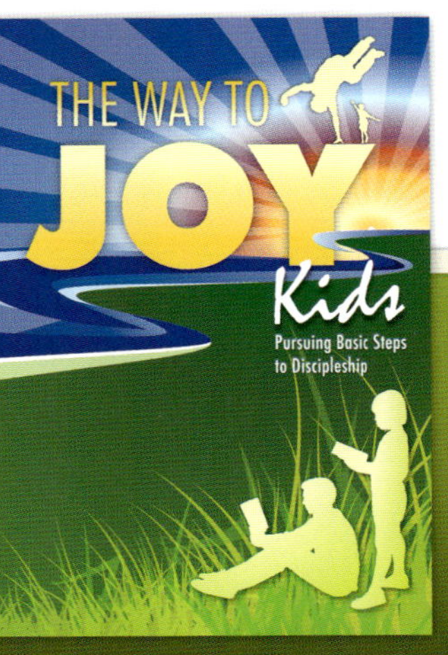

The Way to Joy–Kids is a basic discipleship resource for kids ages 8-12. It is a visual-design and language-level adapted version of **The Way to Joy**. A free (downloadable) Leader's Guide is available.

The Author

After living and working overseas for 23 years as church-planting missionaries, **Gil Thomas** and his wife, Denise, now live in central Pennsylvania. He works and travels as an international trainer, but considers influencing his grandchildren as job one. Also by Gil: *Gaining Ground with Good Soil* and *Kids Sing the Story of Hope* which can both be ordered from www.GoodSoil.com.

The Illustrators

Lars Justinen is the creative director and co-founder of GoodSalt.com. He has worked as an illustrator and publication designer for more than 25 years and has painted thousands of illustrations for national publishers such as McGraw Hill, Scholastic Books, Focus on the Family, Public Television, Lifeway, and Pacific Press, winning national and international awards for his work. His wife, Kim, is also a prolific illustrator of Christian children's books and magazines. They enjoy country living in the Pacific Northwest.

Although **Steve Creitz** was born and reared in the Colorado Rockies, he has traveled and lived all across the US, and has spent time doing mission service in Thailand and Zambia. He received his Masters of Fine Arts from the Academy of Art University, focusing his thesis project on images from Bible prophecy. He also studied for two years with American Impressionists and Realists at the Lyme Academy of Fine Arts in Old Lyme, Connecticut. He lives with his wife, two daughters, an old Jack Russell, and a hamster named Peaches outside Boise, Idaho.

Marcus Mashburn painted the images on pages 195 and 199 and **Aric Nicholson** painted the image on page 201.